PERSONS IN COMMUNITY

PERSONS IN COMMUNITY

Theological Voices from the Pastorate

Edited by

WILLIAM H. LAZARETH

William B. Eerdmans Publishing Company
Grand Rapids, Michigan / Cambridge, U.K.

Wm. B. Eerdmans Publishing Co.
255 Jefferson Ave. S.E., Grand Rapids, Michigan 49503 /
P.O. Box 163, Cambridge CB3 9PU U.K.

Printed in the United States of America

09 08 07 06 05 04 7 6 5 4 3 2 1

Library of Congress Cataloging-in-Publication Data

Persons in community: theological voices from the pastorate /
edited by William H. Lazareth.
p. cm.
Includes bibliographical references.
ISBN 0-8028-2203-7 (pbk.: alk. paper)
1. Man (Christian theology) I. Lazareth, William Henry, 1928-

BT701.3.P47 2004
233′.5 — dc22

2004040903

www.eerdmans.com

Contents

PREFACE

The Recovery of Theology in the Service of the Church

The presupposition underlying this research project is that the so-called "crisis of the church" is neither organizational nor programmatic, but theological. The crisis *of* the church is simply the public face of the crisis *in* the church, which is essentially a crisis of faith.

The Crisis in the Church

There are many studies by social scientists of the phenomenology of this crisis. These studies have been useful and suggestive as to the dimensions and proportions of the problem, but they have seldom touched the heart of the matter. The heart of the matter is the loss of the church's identity as a theological community, occasioned by the distance at which the church lives from the source and sources of its faith and life. The heart of the matter, in the language of faith, is the apparent inability of the contemporary church to answer the question that Jesus put to his disciples long ago, "But who do you say that I am?"

The renewal of the church, now as always, is accomplished by the power of the Holy Spirit and is received as a gift of God. If history is any indication, however, the gift of renewal is most frequently given when the church places itself within the realm of possibility, i.e. in the context of those means of grace by which, according to the Old and New Testaments, the Spirit works.

Thus the renewal of the church begins, at least on the human level, with the recovery of those sources and practices that historically have enabled people to encounter and to be encountered by "the grace of our Lord Jesus Christ, the love of God, and the communion of the Holy Spirit."

The renewal of the church may be anticipated when witness is borne through preaching, teaching, pastoral care, and church administration to the gospel of what God has done in and through Jesus Christ. The persuasiveness of the Christian message, when accompanied by the power of the Spirit, is in the power of its articulation to render a more convincing account of the facts of life, to make more sense out of life, and to give more meaning to life than do other alternatives.

The church is often assisted but never renewed by such things as management skills, goal-setting processes, reorganization, public relations, or conflict management. The church waits most faithfully for the gift of new life when it recovers its identity as a theological community and attends to those sources and practices that are the promised means by which God creates, sustains, and preserves the church.

The Separation of Theology and Church

A significant part of the current crisis in the church is the hiatus between academic theology as an intellectual discipline and ecclesial theology as a confessional stance. The achievement of a high level of competence and specialization in theological education requires a certain degree of proficiency in rational analysis, as well as the mastery of languages, texts, ideas, cultures, and extensive bibliographies. It also requires the maintenance of a certain critical distance in order to distinguish the more from the less true. The bridging of the gap between the academic study of theology and the confessional theology of the church, between the critical distance that rational analysis requires and the profound commitment that Christian witness requires, is not easy and is accomplished only with great skill.

Furthermore, there is a tendency on the part of many denominational theological seminaries, which live in proximity to secular institutions of higher education, to become centers of religious studies. Seminary faculty are increasingly educated in graduate schools of secular universities and are often called to teaching positions in denominational institutions with little knowledge of the theological tradition in which they are to teach. Seminary teachers increasingly write not for the church, but for other professionals in the "guild." Thus the primary purpose of the theological seminary — to prepare pastors for the theological vocation of preaching, teaching, and pastoral care — is undercut by the guild, the priority of which is not that of maintaining the identity of the Christian church.

As might be expected given these circumstances, there has been a sharp decline of the pastor-scholar both in seminary faculties and in the ministry of congregations. The movement from seminary faculty to the ministry of a congregation, and conversely from congregation to classroom, has all but ceased. The result is a relatively new phenomenon in American church life: the profound separation between serious theological work and congregational life.

The Trivialization of the Church

One of the legacies of continental Protestant Christianity is the subordination of questions concerning polity and program to convictions concerning the essence of the church. It began not simply with the question, "How can I find the gracious God?" or "What is the meaning of life?" but with questions concerning the nature of the church, such as "What is the essence of the true church?" and "What are the marks by which it may be recognized?" Questions about polity and boundaries were always secondary to the conviction that the church is the people of God, constituted by the Word of God. Other ecclesiologies approach the essence of the church in other ways, such as the Roman Catholic, Anglican, and representatives of the Anabaptist tradition. But in one way or another, each would confess that the church, unique among all other constructs, is a profoundly theological reality.

The Protestant Reformers also had a clear understanding of the ordained minister. None would have suggested that the ordained ministry as such is essential to the church, only the Word of God heard in faith and obeyed in love. But they knew full well that the minister fulfilled an important office for the well-being of the church, namely that of preaching, teaching, and exercising pastoral care in the context of a Christian congregation. The task of the minister was the theological task of proclamation, explication, and application of the Word of God. The expectation was that, through such service, God would act to gather, establish, and empower the church. Once again, other ecclesiologies would confess that the ordained ministry is essential to the existence of the church. But all would agree that the minister's task is theological in nature, not merely organizational or primarily institutional.

A striking fact about the church in our time is that where ministers pursue their calling as church theologians with energy, intelligence, imagination, and love, the church lives . . . and where they do not, the church tends to be trivialized and languishes. A vital church possesses an institutional sense of self that distinguishes it from a civic club, social agency, political party, or self-help organization; and it does not confuse its minister with a social change agent, therapist, or entertainer. One might well document the fact that the crisis in the church parallels the loss of theological identity by the church and the shift in its understanding of the minister from that of pastor-theologian to that of chief executive officer. Hence the recovery of a substantive doctrine of the ordained ministry as a theological vocation, and a strategy for the formation and support of the pastor as theologian and scholar in preaching, teaching, pastoral care, and administration, are crucial for the renewal of the church and for the revitalization of contemporary Christian communities.

The Center of Theological Inquiry as Servant of the Church

The proposal to establish a center for advanced theological research was first advanced by President James I. McCord at a meeting of the Board of Trustees of Princeton Theological Seminary in 1962. "If the age in which we are living is one of transition and revolution, and if the shape of things to come cannot be predicted," he said, "surely the church ought to have some men and women who are giving intense thought at the deepest level to the church's theology, strategy, and mission in the age that is evolving."

After fifteen years of discussion and planning, a Center of Theological Inquiry was established in Princeton, New Jersey as a separate corporation, not under the control of any denomination or seminary, to inquire at the post-graduate level into the relationship between theological and non-theological disciplines, including both the human and natural sciences; to inquire into the relationship between diverse religious traditions, particularly the Christian and non-Christian, Western and non Western; to inquire into the present state of religious and quasi-religious consciousness in the modern world; and to examine other facets of religion in the modern world as may be appropriate to supplement these inquiries.

It was not intended that the Center should focus on religion in general or that it should undertake its task apart from the faith and life of the ecumenical church. To the contrary, the Center was intended as an expression of the claims and commitments of catholic Christianity to the uniqueness of Jesus Christ; the biblical concern for the redemption of individuals, societies, and the entire creation; and the service of God with the life of the mind. The assumption underlying its existence is that God is the Source and Author of all truth; that truth arrived at in any discipline is not inimical to faith in God; that where faith and reason seem to clash, either reason has been distorted or faith misunderstood and misrepresented.

Over one hundred Protestant, Catholic and Jewish scholars, representing various non-theological as well as the traditional theological disciplines, have undertaken periods of residency at the Center to pursue their research projects. A like number have been involved in consultations, conferences, and seminars sponsored by the Center on such topics as theology and science, Calvin and the visual arts, eschatology, globalization, and biblical authority. The Center seeks to fulfill its founders' vision by being a context in which theology will have to cope in the coming years, and to explore the resources upon which theology may call for so doing.

One issue yet to be addressed, however, is that of dissemination. The Center of Theological Inquiry is committed to the proposition that theology is not true to itself when it is simply an academic discipline, that Christian theology, being by definition incarnational, cannot be done in isolation from the church or the world. It seeks to foster interdisciplinary theological research whereby the faith of the church engages and is engaged by the various forces which shape the culture of which it is a part, e.g. non-theological disciplines, such as science, other philosophies of life and religious traditions.

How might interdisciplinary dialogue, such as that fostered by the Center, gain access to the mind and heart of the church, broaden its theological horizons, and inform its mission in the world? How is the church to recover its identity as a theological community of faith and hope as well as love? What can be done about the separation of theology and church? What role might the Center play in the renewal of the church in our time?

The Pastor-Theologian Program

Assisting us to address this current crisis in the church and in theology, the Lilly Endowment Inc. made a major grant to the Center of Theological Inquiry in support of a new venture in ecumenical theological education. A *Pastor-Theologian Program* would seek to focus attention on the ordained ministry as a theological vocation and on the church as a theological community. We were acting on the conviction that in all denominations there are pastors of exceptional theological scholarship, who lack only the time, context and encouragement for such pursuits, and that on their emergence as a formative influence the renewal of the church depended. They would be further equipped, while in the church's active service, to obey the apostolic admonition to be ready to answer all who ask about "a reason for the hope" that gives life to the church (I Pet. 3:15).

The Center's grant proposal rested on the assumption that a ministry of theological substance is of crucial importance for the renewal of the church. It fully acknowledges the role and place of theological seminaries and divinity schools in preparing men and women for the ordained ministry, but it also contends that additional structures of intellectual development must be in place if the pastor-theologian model of ministry is to be an instrument of the continuing reformation and renewal of the church. Participating pastors, as recommended by church and seminary leaders, would therefore be drawn ecumenically from congregations of various churches throughout the country.

A standard annual curriculum was established. In each academic year, the sixty-person group completed fifteen regional seminars, comprising three sessions of three days' duration each in different locations within five regional areas (Northeast, Southeast, North Central, South Central, West). All five groups expressed a growing sense of common purpose and mutual trust as the three parallel rounds of seminars progressed. Variety was provided by the circulation of eighteen academic resource persons (seminary and university professors). Thematic continuity was achieved through critical group analyses of provided common texts. A concluding annual conference integrated all the members of the regions with an international and interdisciplinary team of teaching professors who were completing their own CTI-related research on the same theme.

"Reading the Bible in Faith" (1998-99)

The research of the first year of the program focused on the theme of "Reading the Bible in Faith." Special attention was given to the interpretation of two key texts: the binding of Isaac (Gen. 22) and the Passion of Christ (Matt. 26–27). The texts were chosen because they directed attention to theological issues that are crucial for the church's preaching and teaching in our time: theology of the cross, faithful suffering and death, obedience, the relation of the Old and New Testaments, and the identity, purpose, and action of the Triune God.

We believed that the church's current confusion is related to its loss of the capacity to read biblical texts such as these in profound engagement with church tradition. We hoped to help promote the recovery of practices of "Christian reading." Moreover, we expected that these conversations would generate a range of teaching and writing projects which could eventually be shared with one another and the wider public. That hope was eventually realized in publishing a representative cross-section of the members' excerpted essays in the first volume of this series: William H. Lazareth (ed.), *Reading the Bible in Faith: Theological Voices from the Pastorate,* Eerdmans, 2001.

"Theology, Science and the Future" (1999-2000)

The research of the 1999-2000 academic year centered on the theme of "Theology, Science and the Future." Capitalizing on the general public's millennialist interest and concerns surrounding the year 2000, we concentrated theologically on the central issues: What can Christians hope for? How do signs of God's reign shape the church's faith and life today? Where can we find the power to prevail in a culture that faces unprecedented forces of both life and death? Our aim was to develop a realistic eschatology that was both doctrinally faithful and contemporaneously intelligible. The method was to explore the interrelation of the natural and social sciences with various biblical, theological, and ethical traditions.

The same pattern of regional seminars and a concluding annual conference enabled the members to benefit from a wide range of academic and denominational exchanges in their preparation of twenty-page research papers or projects on a subject related to the year's general theme. Excerpts of the results were again editorially collated and published as the second volume of this series: William H. Lazareth (ed.), *Hope for Your Future: Theological Views from the Pastorate,* Eerdmans, 2002.

"Theological Anthropology" (2000-2001)

What does it mean to be a person? What are the essential features of human personhood as revealed in Holy Scripture, explicated in Christian doctrine, and critically related to recent developments in modern philosophy, science, and the arts? Which are the basic insights and exemplars from the ecumenical Christian tradition that can still provide guidance and inspiration for the human creatures' quest for personal integrity, along with justice, peace, and freedom in community life? These were among the chief questions posed for the research of the program's third year of operation.

Once again the sixty-person group completed fifteen regional seminars. Variety was provided by the circulation of fifteen academic resource persons (seminary and university professors). Thematic continuity was achieved through the critical analyses of the provided nine common texts:

Barth, Karl, *Church Dogmatics,* III, 2 (Edinburgh: T&T Clark, 1960).

Burns, L. Patout, *Theological Anthropology* (Philadelphia: Fortress, 1981).

Graff, Ann Elizabeth O'Hara, ed., *In the Embrace of God* (Maryknoll, N.Y.: Orbis, 1995).

Jenson, Robert W., *Systematic Theology,* II (New York: Oxford, 1997).

Murphy, Nancy, et al., eds., *Whatever Happened to the Soul?* (Minneapolis: Fortress Press, 1998).

Percy, Walker, *The Message in the Bottle: How Queer Man Is, How Queer Language Is, and What One Has to Do with the Other* (New York: Picador, 2000).

Reuther, Rosemary Radford, *Women and Redemption* (Minneapolis: Fortress Press, 1998).

Schnelle, Udo, *The Human Condition* (Minneapolis: Fortress Press, 1996).
Wolff, Hans-Walter, *Anthropology of the Old Testament* (Minneapolis: Fortress, 1996).

The lectures and discussions of the third annual national conference further exposed the pastors of the five regions to the interplay of theological anthropology (Robert Jenson, Center of Theological Inquiry, Princeton, and R. Kendall Soulen, Wesley Theological Seminary) with a variety of current secular disciplines: culture (Carver Yu, China Graduate School of Theology), science (Wentzel van Huyssteen, Princeton Theological Seminary), fine arts (Marilyn Chandler McEntyre, Westmont College), politics (Jean Bethke Elshtain, University of Chicago), and artificial intelligence (Anne Foerst, St. Bonaventure University).

Expanding the Discussions

A complete roster of all clergy participants in the year's program activities is provided at the end of this book. Included in their number are the authors of the excerpted articles edited for publication in this volume. While these blocs of material are admittedly both short and taken out of context, they nevertheless do contribute far more to a lively, multi-voiced discussion than would the total arguments of their authors' much longer original essays. Each chapter is opened with an editor's introduction that briefly integrates the theme-oriented excerpts. We have intentionally retained the authors' diversity in style and structure. In short, the format allows for more pastor-theologians to make their distinctive contributions to what is essentially an ecumenical group effort. Mary Rae Rogers deserves credit for her careful work on the manuscript during its various stages of preparation.

We publish this book, therefore, both as a record of the Center's initial stewardship, and as a cordial invitation for readers, especially other pastor-theologians in local congregations, to join us by extension in this and other similar publications of annual discussions already projected for future years. We do so with deep gratitude to the Lilly Endowment Inc. for its generous financial assistance and helpful staff support in our joint endeavor with Eerdmans to strengthen outstanding pastor-theologians for leading the people of God in the mission of the church of Jesus Christ in and for the world.

Wallace M. Alston, Jr.
Director, Center of Theological Inquiry

William H. Lazareth
Program Associate, Pastor-Theologian Program

PART ONE

IN GOD'S IMAGE

CHAPTER I

Biblical Anthropology

Introduction

We do not begin at the beginning. It is always something of a shock for the pious reader to learn how very late an author of Genesis 1 began to write, "In the beginning." Indeed, that is true not only of the multiple millennia of the physical universe, but also even of the religious world of the ancient Jews. The accounts of God's creation of the world and of humanity therein were compiled of earlier orally preserved traditions relatively late in the composition of the Old Testament itself, likely during the exile or early post-exilic Jewish community in Jerusalem only some six centuries before the birth of Christ.

Moreover, to these archeological and textual findings of modern biblically critical scholarship, we must also now add the theological exegetical consensus that the anthropology of the New Testament begins not with God's old creation of the first Adam in Genesis but rather with the new creation of the final Adam in Jesus, the world's Lord and Savior. The Gospel is first centered in Christology and only then governs a coherent anthropology. This lays the evangelical foundation for the church's still later creedal confession that Jesus Christ is God's gracious incarnation, "true man" (human) as well as "true God" (divine), among us. That is why our opening essays in biblical anthropology read the witness of the Old Testament in light of the faith of the New. But they themselves do not agree on the Gospel's center.

David Henderson traces this movement "from solution to plight" in Paul's proclamation of the Gospel in his Epistle to the Romans. The apostle's soteriologically determined description of the human condition highlights Romans 7:14-25. Throughout Christian history, however, this passage has been variously interpreted in three different ways: (1) as an autobiographical account of Paul's pre-conversion experience; (2) as a general description of human experience under the law apart from Christ; and (3) as Paul's own experience as a believer, which by implication also applies to all other Christians. Whatever choice is made, of course, must be organically related to the remainder of Paul's argument on Christian soteriology, its resultant anthropology, and the relation of the messages of the Old and New Testaments. The author explores the three options and offers his own concluding judgment.

Deborah R. Clemens proceeds very differently with a Christological, rather than Christocentric, reading of God's image in Genesis 1. She combines a low view of sin and redemption as foundational for an authentic Christian anthropology. The claimed New Testament resources on creation are such non-Pauline texts as John 1, Hebrews 1, and II Peter 3. Persons never have been the image of God; Christ alone is. We only demean Christ when we assume that God and human creatures share certain characteristics. Actually, the Hebrew concept of what it means to be human comes not from Genesis, but from the Jews' liberation story in Exodus. This is allegedly confirmed by Christ's teaching in John: to be truly human "is to be organically and essentially and eternally living in Christ" as the liberating Son of God. What, then, of Genesis 1:26? "Let *us* make humankind in *our* image" (in the plural) should rightly be interpreted as a trinitarian passage with Christ as the divine agent of creation. "To be created in God's image means to be created in Christ, nothing more and nothing less." It follows for the author that Christ's ultimate purpose in his later incarnation was not to atone for the human's lost image of God in the Fall, but that God "became human so that the entire universe might be reconciled into divine perfection." The Creator aimed at forming union with created beings. Thereby we are called to engage in "imitating the image" of Christ's demonstrated self-giving love among us. We will fail, but God's grace will prevail.

Allen C. McSween, Jr., next reviews the Scripture's narrative descriptions, rather than propositional definitions, of human sin. Genesis depicts for him the original breach in relations among God, human creatures, and the rest of the created order. David's sin with Bathsheba provides a vivid narrative backdrop for Psalm 51 in particular, and the entire Psalmody in general. Paul's proclamation of Jesus Christ as the righteous last Adam, who overcomes the corporate sin of humankind in the first Adam, interrelates Romans 5–6 with Genesis 1–3. Hence, in light of the human's distinctive call to image God, the author admonishes his fellow preachers to stay close to the "profound realism of Scripture" in depicting human sin and divine grace.

The 51st Psalm is analyzed by Albert Keller in his investigation of the identity of the "I" who prays this psalm of penitent contrition. This is especially needed in view of the psalm-prayer's common use in synagogues and churches today. He responds at four levels. First, some have identified it with King David. Second, others have dated it more recently with the Davidic-related post-exilic Jewish community in Jerusalem. Third, a deep response has come from the person and community in Christ beginning six centuries later. Finally, in our own day especially, a fourth response may be made in the context of evolutionary biology. Here persons are seen as being shaped by a critical coherence with a scientific understanding of humanity as part of created nature. Consequently, the sciences — neurobiology, evolutionary psychology, human behavioral ecology, among others — must be accepted as partners in current anthropological dialogue.

1. *Human Being and the Law of Sin*

David Henderson

As Udo Schnelle argues, the starting point for the development of a biblical anthropology is the Scriptures themselves, specifically as they give witness to God's saving act in Jesus Christ proclaimed in the New Testament.[1] Schnelle points out that the New Testament does not begin with the human condition and work its way towards an understanding of God's solution; rather, the New Testament authors begin with God's salvific action in Jesus Christ, and proceed to describe humanity in light of this event. As Schnelle puts it, Christology and soteriology are prior to anthropology, insofar as our understanding of human being is rooted in God's action in Jesus Christ. Human being is defined by Jesus Christ, in light of his person and work — not the other way around.

In what follows, I shall be attempting to show how Paul, in his Epistle to the Romans, argues precisely in this way, that is, *from solution to plight.* Specifically, I shall be looking at Romans 7:14-25 and its particular description of the human condition as it relates to the overall context of Paul's argument. Issues such as law and grace, sin and righteousness, bondage and freedom come into play as Paul explicates the impact and meaning of Christ's saving work in relation to human being.

For centuries, much debate and controversy has centered on Romans 7:14-25. Varying interpretations of this key passage have yielded understandings of Paul's theology as a whole, and this text has been, and continues to be, seen as pivotal in understanding Paul's anthropology and soteriology. Opinion surrounding the meaning of this passage has been divided in three ways: (1) Romans 7:14-25 gives Paul's autobiographical account of his own pre-conversion experience; (2) the passage is not strictly autobiographical, but describes human experience in general apart from Christ, under the law; (3) Paul's own experience even as a believer is being described, and thus by implication applies to Christian experience in general. Such has been the focus of the debate, yet as many commentators point out, the question of pre-Christian versus Christian experience depicted in Romans 7 has often eclipsed the more substantive issues at hand. Whether Paul is describing pre-Christian or Christian experience is, of course, an important question; but it must be viewed only in relation to prior issues such as the overall purpose and intent of the argument contained in the passage, its relation to the epistle as a whole, and an understanding of key terms, themes, and motifs which Paul employs in the passage. To allow the question of whether Paul describes pre-Christian or Christian experience to be asked prior to an examination of these issues may create certain presuppositions, which greatly impair the exegetical task.

Romans 7:14-25 is an integral part of Paul's overall exposition of the new relationship of the person to God in Christ. Some scholars regard 7:7-25 as an excursus on Paul's part — an interruption in the flow of his argument; yet a close examination of Paul's overall argument reveals the passage to be logically tied to the previous discussion in chapters 5 and 6, as well as that which follows in chapter 8.

Beginning with 5:12, Paul proceeds to outline the character of the new relationship of the person to God in Christ in terms of participation — participation in Adam has meant sin and death; participation in Christ means righteousness and life. The groundwork for chapters 6, 7, and 8 is laid in these verses (5:12-21). Paul establishes humanity's solidarity in Adam, that is, humanity's participation in sin as a structure of power that rules through death. He then contrasts Adam's sin with the grace given in Jesus Christ, which brings righteousness and life. Involved in this discussion is a third element, law. Paul has already alluded to the role of law in 3:20 and 3:21, and again does so in 5:13 and 5:20. Verses 20 and 21 of chapter 5 serve as a prolegomenon to chapters 6, 7, and 8.

In chapters 6 and 7 Paul discusses (1) the relationship between sin and grace (6:1-14); (2) the relationship between law and grace (6:15–7:6); and (3) the relationship between law and sin (7:7-25).[2] Each of these discussions is introduced by a rhetorical question in diatribe form, in which Paul draws the obvious (but incorrect) conclusion from the previous discussion. To each of these questions Paul gives his corrective reply, and goes on to give an exposition of his rebuttal.

In response to the question, "Are we to continue in sin that grace may abound?" Paul describes the character of new life in Christ in terms of participation. Participation in Christ's death and resurrection through baptism is death to sin and life to God (6:10-11). Paul here expounds the relationship of sin to grace — the radical discontinuity that exists between a life lived in sin and a life lived in Christ. Whereas Paul had previously dealt with the problem of sin relationally, he now begins to describe the problem structurally or ontologically. Sin is seen as a structure of power that reigns in our mortal bodies (v. 12), making its claim on our lives and leading us to wickedness and death. Participation in Christ means freedom from sin's domination and from the rule of death itself. In verse 14, Paul relates the domination of sin to the law, and thus must again avoid the false inference that could be drawn from his argument.

Paul again asks the rhetorical question, "Are we to sin because we are not under law but under grace?" (6:15). His answer is, again, an emphatic no, and he goes on to characterize human existence as slavery — bondage to sin, or bondage to God (vv. 17, 18, 22). But what of the law? Paul has already implied that the Christian is free from the law (6:14), but he must now explain more fully what he means. He does this as the argument begun in 6:15 continues to 7:7. The thrust of this latter portion of the argument (including the problematic analogy from marriage) is that the Christian, through participation in Christ, has died to the law and henceforth belongs to another — to Christ. In verse 5, Paul comments on the close relationship between the law and sin, which he will continue to expound in the remainder of chapter 7. In verse 6, he comments on the new life of the Spirit, which frees one from the sin-dominated law. This new life in the Spirit will be fully discussed by Paul in Chapter 8.

Romans 7:14-25 thus is an exposition of the relationship of sin to the law, beginning with the diatribe, "What then shall we say? That the law is sin?" (v. 7). Some commentators, as previously mentioned, have held that 7:7-25 is an excursus — a break in Paul's argument wherein he offers a defense of the law. However, in the overall context of Paul's argument as outlined above, it seems rather to be the case that Paul's focus is primarily on sin as a structure of power that is able to overcome even the law. The passage in this light is not an apology for the law, but rather a description of the power of sin.

In 7:7-13, Paul gives an account of the function of the law in its relation to sin. Here, sin is depicted as the force, the structure of power that has made use of the law, which is itself holy, and turned its intent towards evil. The remainder of the chapter is a further description of sin's domination of the self that recognizes the right action, but is unable to accomplish it. Chapter 7 becomes a prelude to chapter 8, where indwelling sin and its power over the person (and the law) are replaced by the indwelling Spirit (8:9-10).

As stated at the outset, the focus of the debate over Romans 7:14-25 has been on the question of whose experience is being described. Who is the ego? Following Dunn's division of the opinion into three categories, we shall examine the arguments in support of each interpretation.[3]

The first of the interpretations that Dunn identifies, namely, the view that Paul in Romans 7:14-25 describes his own pre-conversion experience, has largely been forsaken by most contemporary scholars in light of W. G. Kümmel's monograph *Römer 7*, published in 1929.[4] One proponent of this view was C. H. Dodd. Dodd argues that the "I" of Romans 7:14-25 bears the same autobiographical significance as the "I" statements in Galatians 2:19-21 and Philippians 3:7-14.[5] Dodd goes on to argue, based on the context of the passage, that Paul describes his own inner struggle with sin and the law prior to the Damascus road experience.

The second position Dunn identifies sees Romans 7:14-25 as not strictly autobiographical, but as a description of pre-conversion experience in general. Proponents of this view (including Bultmann, Käsemann, Achtemeier, and Kümmel) see vv. 7-11 as referring to Adam's experience, as his experience is paradigmatic of human experience in general. This view harmonizes vv. 7-11 with 5:12, which speaks of Adam's prototypical sin and its effects. For Käsemann, Paul's use of "I" emphasizes universal participation in Adam.[6] Romans 7:14-25 then becomes the confessional statement of all that participate in Adam and have not yet participated in Christ.

The third alternative interpretation takes the passage at face value, and treats it as not only Paul's own present experience, but as the experience of every human person *in light of Christ.* Proponents of this view include Nygren, Dunn, Bruce, Cranfield, Murray, as well as Augustine, Luther, Calvin, and Barth. Nygren argues that chapters 5, 6, 7, and 8 are all concerned with the Christian life, and that chapter 7 addresses the question of the Christian's relationship to the law. The Christian's life, lived in the eschatological tension of the "already/not yet," is thus torn between will and action. The Christian lives simultaneously in two aeons — the old and the new, and this is the tension Paul describes in Romans 7:14-25. Nygren refers to Galatians 5:17 as an example of Paul's treatment of this same issue.[7] Cranfield follows Nygren, and states that Romans 7 describes one aspect of Christian life, the continuous struggle between the spirit and the flesh — while chapter 8 describes Christian life from the perspective of life in the Spirit.[8]

In my own attempt to interpret this problematic passage, I return to my original assertion that one cannot begin with the question of whether Paul is describing Christian or pre-Christian experience, and then attempt to get at the meaning of the text. Rather, it is necessary to view the passage within the context of Paul's overall argument. Viewed in this way, it becomes clear that Paul is not so much concerned to describe what we would call "Christian" or "pre-Christian" experience as he is to expose the radical nature of sin's power over human existence and the overwhelming power of God's grace in Christ to conquer sin. In Romans 7:14-25, the effects of sin's bondage are made manifest, and the law is revealed to be powerless against it. Romans 7:25a declares the only possible deliverance from this bondage, echoing 6:14ff, and chapter 8 goes on to describe the character of life lived in the Spirit.

There is no doubt that Christians live in the tension of the "already/not yet," and Paul certainly describes this tension in such texts as Galatians 5:17; yet, he goes on even in this passage to affirm that "if you are led by the Spirit you are not under the law." Even the dialectic of the indicative and imperative of Romans 6 attests to the fact that such a tension exists.

The paradox is, however, that it is only from the standpoint of grace that one becomes acutely aware of the tension. It is only in light of the radical nature of God's grace in Jesus Christ that we become fully conscious of the gravity of our condition, and our inability to free ourselves from sin's bondage. Even from the perspective of faith (or, we should say, only from the standpoint of faith) are we made to realize the battle within us between flesh and spirit, a battle that is exposed after conversion, and we are led all the more to throw ourselves upon the mercy of God's grace in Christ. In this life, our existence continues to be qualified by the power of sin and death, as we "live in the flesh." As Barth puts it, to live without this tension that Paul describes in chapter 7 would be resurrection life, a life we have yet to fully enter — a life that only Christ has fully realized.

From the standpoint of biblical anthropology, or more specifically, Christian anthropology, Romans 7:14-25 stands as a clear statement of the gospel truth that our humanity, our existence is defined and judged by Jesus Christ, in light of his person and work. I reiterate what Schnelle has said, that Christology and soteriology are prior to anthropology. What it means to be human is understood only as the Cross of Christ exposes the plight of the human condition and our utter powerlessness in the face of sin and death. This leads us unavoidably to an entirely pessimistic view of human life and potential *apart from God's grace in Jesus Christ.* The radicalness of God's grace in Christ exposes the radicalness of sin's power over us, and of our absolute reliance on Christ's atoning work. Much contemporary understanding of the human person, derived as it is from social sciences, is far removed from the New Testament portrayal of the human person. Insofar as we begin with our experience of human being, rather than with a Christological and soteriological foundation as Paul does, then we not only will have a false understanding of what it means to be human; we are also left with a diminished understanding of Christ and his saving work.

2. *Christ the Image*

Deborah Rahn Clemens

The Image of God

At first glance, the biblical concept of humanity being created in the divine image appears to be an argument used to elevate our species. Scientists scoff at the notion that *Homo sapiens* are any different than their animal cousins except for their brain capacity and command of language. There is no laboratory evidence for God's reflection in one of our kind. Nevertheless, Christians, Jews, and Muslims insist humans are created in God's image (Genesis 1:26). It's quite another thing to determine what this basic biblical affirmation might mean.

The most common assumption created by this doctrine is that God and people must share certain characteristics. Because it is far easier to note human traits than it is to make definitive statements about God, individuals have collected a number of virtues known to exist in our species and conclude that these must mirror the divine personality. Therefore, since humans at their best are loving and nurturing and creative, we portray the Creator of the universe as like us in these ways. Actually what we are doing by this way of reasoning is placing God in our own image. How do we explain our selfish, hateful, greedy traits? We do so by proposing that such attributes were acquired only in our sinful state. They are not shared by God. They are a distortion of God's image. They look like Adam and Eve.

If this then is the theory, that we look like God, or at least that we share in God's finer traits, then what does this say to a theology of human failing? Either we must conclude that the image is so distorted by sin that the concept has no impact on human reality today. So why continue to claim it? Or, we might argue that there is something about this image thing that we are ontologically, and therefore naturally capable of having. Naturally, then, we can love. Naturally we can be caring. Naturally we can be creative. Such claims lead us to teach that naturally we can be like God. I thought this kind of thinking got Adam and Eve in trouble in the first place.

To carry forth this line of reasoning is also to suggest that human beings ought to be able to accomplish the good virtues we seek to accomplish. Pelagius would applaud! Try hard enough, do good enough, cooperate with grace and, lo and behold, we can influence the outcome of salvation history. Failed human beings, however, serve as a corrective to this interpretation of the *imago Dei,* at least if it is the best in humans that reflect God's being.

Classical descriptions of the *imago Dei* focus our concerns a bit differently. Philo is credited for associating human reason with the divine image.[9] He saw the Logos as that in the mind of God which can be replicated in human beings. Philo did not equate the Logos with the fullness of God but understood it to be an important attribute of the deity. Rationality — a rational human soul more specifically — was then interpreted as the stuff that made humans superior to the rest of created beings and able to "know" God. From this point on classical teaching suggests that reason and intelligence are our godlike qualities. Therefore we are justified in dominating all the other less intelligent animals on the planet and should be able to find God via theological logic. In light of human failure, however, we must acknowledge that plenty of us are let down by our intelligence. If intelligence is the closest attribute we have to God, what of the nuclear scientists? The smarter we are, the more righteous we are?

Added to Philo's argument for intelligence is the partner trait in classic descriptions of the image: free will. Free will is that which enables us to choose between good and evil. Free will is that which allows us to make our decision for God or for the devil. It is by free will that we sin, and it is by free will that we repent. To be in the image of God is to have free will. This gets God off the hook concerning the source of evil. It isn't God's fault that people choose badly. The ultimate good must be therefore in the ability to choose evil. It explains why there can be evil nuclear scientists.

But are we really free? Free to do what? Free to opt against God? What is the alternative? A theology of human failure reminds us that humans are dependent. We are not free if freedom means separation from God. We are not free to fully control our bodies, our minds, our future, our family, or our environment. If free will enabled Adam and Eve to lose the garden, why would we want to hold it up as a gift from God? On the outside chance that with our free will we will do the opposite? Fat chance.

One of the problems we have in interpreting what it means to be in the image of God, I think, is that we begin with the Genesis narrative. Genesis is not the beginning. Genesis is not the beginning in Jewish self-understanding. Neither is Genesis the beginning of who we know ourselves to be in Christianity. The Hebrew concept of what it means to be a human being grows out of the Exodus, the liberation story. God set Moses straight:

> I am the LORD, and I will bring you out from under the burdens of the Egyptians, and I will deliver you from their bondage, and I will redeem you with an outstretched arm and with great acts of judgment, and I will take you for My people, and I will be your God: And you shall know that I am the LORD your God, who has brought you out from under the burdens of the Egyptians. And I will bring you into the land, which I swore to give to Abraham, to Isaac, and to Jacob; I will give it to you for a possession. I am the LORD. (Exodus 6:6-8)

This first and foremost defines for the Jew what it means to be human. It means being dependent on God. It means having a relationship with Him. It means being freed from our burdens. It means having a heritage and a homeland. It does not mean we are intelligent or that we possess freedom.

The Christian concept of what it means to be human comes directly from Jesus:

> As the living Father sent me, and I live because of the Father, so whoever eats me will live because of me. (John 6:57)

> If you continue in my Word, you are truly my disciples, and you will know the truth, and the truth will make you free. (John 8:31-32)

> My sheep hear my voice, and I know them, and they follow me; and I give them eternal life, and they shall never perish, and no one shall snatch them out of my hand. . . . I and the Father are one. (John 10:27-30)

> I am the resurrection and the life; those who believe in me, even though they die, will live, and everyone who lives and believes in me will never die. (John 11:25-26)

> On that day you will know that I am in my Father and you in me, and I in you. (John 14:20)

> I am the vine; you are the branches. He who abides in me and I in him, he it is that bears much fruit, for apart from me you can do nothing. (John 15:5)

To be human, according to Christ, is to be organically and essentially and eternally living in Christ. By virtue of that life in Christ we are totally dependent on him, freed from our burdens, destined for a homeland, and willed to be united with God the Father in heaven. It does not mean we are intelligent or that we possess freedom.

We are *not* the image of God. And we never have been. There is no justification for us to try to look at ourselves to find God reflected. We are not even the image of God that has become damaged or broken or tarnished. Genesis is truth. Genesis 1:26 is truth telling. Genesis 1:26 is revelation. However, it is not the beginning of our knowledge of God or our understanding of what it means to be human. Once we know Christ, once we know liberation, then we can begin to grasp what it means to be created *in* God's image. To be created *in* God's image is something totally different. It is good news for failed humans.

According to the Genesis passage, God said, "Let us make humankind in our image, according to our likeness" (Genesis 1:26). The plural "us" and the preposition "in" are especially of interest. How can we explain a first person plural pronoun when God himself is speaking? We have a few options. We can attribute this writing to such a primitive tradition that it predates Hebrew monotheism. Surely the Mosaic affirmation of the one true God came somewhere in time after creation. However, editors J, P, and D didn't predate monotheism. It was firmly entrenched when these great foundational myths were recorded. We could decide that the "us" was simply a grammatical error or a textual glitch. Perhaps centuries upon centuries of proofreaders simply missed catching this. Sloppy scribes, you know. We could believe the "us" represents a conversation between God and the angels. Even Karl Barth was attracted to this option.[10]

Perhaps God was consulting the heavenly host throughout creation's process. Of course, we are not told when the angels were created. If Genesis records the order of creation from the least to the greatest, human beings being the culmination, where did these angels come from? Were they created first before heaven, or next? If humans are created in the angelic image, shouldn't we be paying a lot more attention to them? Genesis 1:27 clears up any confusion. It says, "So God created humankind in his image, in the image of God he created them, male and female he created them" (Genesis 1:27). There is no notion of angels in this verse. It is still God's image.

I see only one other option in explaining the "us" from Genesis. That is to interpret this as a Trinitarian passage — to acknowledge the sufficiency and the unity and the community already in the Godhead when the universe was created. To affirm that Christ and the Holy Spirit were also active and had voice in all of revelation. To acknowledge Hebrews 1, John 1, and II Peter 3 as correct: Christ was the agent of creation. The "us" of Genesis refers to Christ and the Holy Spirit. To be created in God's image means to be created in Christ, nothing more and nothing less.

The Purpose of the Incarnation

Whether or not we accept the theory that humans suffer from a tarnished or broken image (which I do not), we still have to consider the relationship in Incarnation and sin. Would God have become human even if we did not sin? Numerous New Testament passages give us the impression that sin is the ultimate first cause of Christ's coming. We read in I Corinthians 15:3, "Christ died for our sins in accordance to scripture." In John 15:13, "There is no greater love than this: to lay down one's life for one's friends." Surely the separation between God and humans has been forever annulled by the Atonement. But this does not satisfy the question as to whether the removal of sins was Christ's ultimate purpose when coming into the created realm. If this were the case, then it would be logical to deduce that sin is the ultimate good: "Let sin abound so that grace may abound." Obviously there is a problem with this argument. It is the brat-that-craves-attention argument: If I am naughty, then Mommy or Daddy will notice. Therefore maybe love can be had by performing evil acts. No, there must be something more and something greater happening in the Incarnation.

Furthermore, as much as we all need to have our sins forgiven, it is not clear whether forgiveness is the right remedy for failed human beings. Does a "failure" need to be forgiven for not succeeding? One would hope not. At the same time, however, a failure definitely needs something not attainable by human effort. A failure no less yearns for a gospel of salvation. The need to know that one is redeemed might conceivably be greater in the failure than in the sinner. For the failure, guilt is often prevalent. Yet, it is unclear as to how to repent or from what to repent. Must one repent of one's own being? This is another impossible solution. For a human to repent of being human is itself a denial of God's creative wisdom.

Why did God become human? Did God become human primarily to undo a human act? This on the face of things seems absurd. It is not enough to demand that God must change God's very being in order to erase sin.[11] There is only one acceptable reason for God himself to form union with created beings. Union between heaven and earth, or more accurately, God and the universe, is totally impossible from the universe's end. The rocks cannot morph, the trees cannot become hybrids, and no free willing, intelligent being can accomplish enough transformation to unite with God. That is unachievable with or without sin! The only possibility for communion among the created and the uncreated is if the uncreated becomes also created. In other words, union is possible only if God would be incarnated.

The traditional office of Mediator assigned to Christ in Catholic teaching is correct but insufficient in explaining the reason for the Incarnation. While it is absolutely true that Christ is the Mediator between the two realms, mediation does not necessarily demand union. The docetic heresies would prove equally as good as a theory for that function. A masquerading God might fool the world. But a masquerading God does not make oneness. God became human so that the entire universe might be reconciled into divine perfection.

If this is the case, then Christ restores more than the garden. Our destiny is greater than a second honeymoon in Eden.[12] Humanity has been granted something more than a scratch-proof appearance of naked Eve and Adam. Christ is more than the handy Mr. Fix-it. He is the new creation.

What does this have to do with a theology of human failure? Everything! It moves the focus away from what humans do to who humans are. We are organically and essentially united with Christ. We are totally dependent on him. We are freed from our burdens. We are destined for a homeland. We are willed to be united eternally with the Godhead. It is all about who we are, not about what we have accomplished.

Imitating the Image

Classic reformation insight reminds that one is saved by grace through faith. Therefore our unsuccessful attempts at being good or working for a righteous cause or striving to be what we believe we are called to be should not affect our status as justified in the eyes of the Deity. The difficulty lies not in the doctrine, but in the application of that truth in absolving the souls of those suffering from the existential angst of failing. In other words, the issue might be, if we are saved by grace, are we also saved in disgrace?

Let us look to Paul, the original articulator of this doctrine, for help in understanding the power of grace in disgrace. Fortunately, the Epistle to the Philippians works directly with this topic. Philippians is one of the most tender and more vulnerable of the Apostle's writings. It was written when Paul was imprisoned and exhausted, and preparing to face the end of his life with an overwhelming sense of being personally defeated. Paul, of course, began his career sure of his actions as a devoted, Pharisaical Jewish man. After his conversion he devoted his life to the mission of establishing churches and molding gospel interpretation. Throughout his career he had to fight to legitimize his apostolic status. He boldly took on Peter, James, and the Jerusalem Christians when he believed they were misinterpreting the place of Jewish tradition. Paul controlled the nascent Gentile congregations with the hand of an autocrat.

In his cell, towards the end of his life, Paul had to come to terms with his own human failings. In Philippians he does not claim apostolic status. Rather he labels himself as a servant. He is no longer a Pharisee, no longer a Jew, no longer an upstanding Roman citizen. In Christian circles themselves he is often despised and attacked. And as an incarcerated man he is unable to preach the gospel and unable to found new churches. Paul is forced to face the question every failure faces: "Who am I now that I am no longer who I thought I was?"

"Who am I," asks the man whose wife walks out after thirty years of marriage, "if I am no longer a husband?"

"Who am I," asks the ice dancer who on the verge of the Olympic games suddenly finds herself without a partner, "if I am no longer a skater?"

"Who am I?" asks the professional drummer who after an automobile accident loses all use of his right hand, "if I am no longer a drummer?"

"Who am I?" asks the woman whose four children were casualties of war, "if I am no longer a mother?"

"Who am I?" asks Paul, "if I am no longer a Pharisee, a Jew, a Christian preacher, a pastor, an apostle of the Lord?"

Paul was also no Stoic. He suffered deeply. He would have preferred to die rather than live, if he had his own personal druthers (Philippians 1:21-22). Yet the overwhelming tenor of the epistle to the Philippians is joy and rejoicing (Philippians 4:4). Paul is able to come to this joy, I believe, only because he came to understand the theology of human failing. He discovered that:

1. What we cannot accomplish, God will bring to completion. (Philippians 1:6)
2. Curiously, the gospel may be advanced even by those who deliberately work against our good causes. (Philippians 1:18)
3. We can fall flat on our faces and still be all right, for Christ will keep us safe. (Philippians 1:19)
4. In Christ we are assured that we will be redeemed and, like Job, know all things will work out for our salvation. (Philippians 2:12-13)
5. Failed efforts are not useless but rather are sacrifices, offerings to the Lord. (Philippians 2:16-18)
6. Even when we cannot accomplish the task, God will send someone else to continue the work. (Philippians 2:19-30)
7. No matter how successful we are, all human achievements are rubbish when compared to the gift of Jesus Christ. What matters is the fact that we belong to Christ. We don't make ourselves acceptable to God; rather, God renders us acceptable because of our faith. Therefore human disgrace is an avenue of grace. It removes the barriers erected by self-pride and praise. (Philippians 3:3-11)
8. Never give up. Leave your failures behind. They don't define you. Move ahead towards the goal. Who are you when you are not whatever you once considered yourself to be? You are a citizen of heaven. (Philippians 3:12-21)

Paul comes to the realization that all human life attests to the sovereignty of God.[13] That testimony is most clearly seen not in the human's triumph, but in the individual's defeat.[14] The Christian who faithfully channels his or her intellect and free will in the service of God will eventually find both come to futility according to worldly standards of success. It is precisely at this point, however, that one witnesses to the power of God most honestly. All human life moves on a continuum from birth to death. In the beginning stages of our lives we as creatures reflect God's gift of creation. We often function as if we were free and autonomous persons, belonging only to ourselves. But this is only an illusion. Through our failures and inevitable loss of freedom we come to realize that we do not belong to ourselves at all but belong and have belonged all along only to Christ Jesus. In our voluntary or involuntary surrender of our autonomy we emerge united with divinity. Each individual human story is a miniature replica of God's purpose for the universe. The continuum from birth to death and resurrection models the continuum from creation to consummation.

Our hope is not in our freedom, though our freedom is real. Freedom, however, is what we have to make of our witness between the two poles of birth and death. It is significant, but our ultimate hope does not lie in it. Our ultimate hope lies in God and in God's purpose. Human limitations therefore are not essential hindrances but ultimate testimonies to the vastness beyond.

Jesus lives in the same continuum from the manger to the cross. He exemplifies what it is to be truly human. He also exemplifies what it is to be truly God:

> Though he was in the form (image) of God, (he) did not regard equality with God as something to be exploited, but emptied himself, taking the form (image) of a slave, being born in human likeness, and being found in human form (image), he humbled himself and became obedient to the point of death — even death on a cross. Therefore God also highly exalted him and gave him the name that is above every name, so that at the name of Jesus every knee should bend, in heaven and on earth and under the earth, and every tongue should confess that Jesus Christ is Lord, to the glory of the Father. (Philippians 2:6-11)

The fact is that God's humanity, true humanity, is recognized not in the one who super-achieves. Jesus failed to win much popular attention. He built no monuments. He established no schools, hospitals, institutions, or charities in his day. He demonstrated no unusual physical strength. He earned no particular regard in his society. He died broke and in disgrace. Yet God's humanity is recognized in the de-humanized Jesus most perfectly.[15]

This tells us something new about God's image. To be in God's image is not to resemble the best in this world, but to conform to one who was emptied of everything but humility. The concept is not in any way degrading. The goal is not simply the physical, or spiritual, or physiological brokenness of persons. The point of imitating Christ is to share in his exaltation. Christ lives and reigns eternally as the second person of the Godhead. He also lives and reigns as the one who is fully God and fully human. Christ's exaltation elevates the entire human species. Anyone created in Him (which means anyone created in God's image) has the potential of being united in glory with Him. Anyone born anew into the incarnate body has the guarantee of that ultimate destination. Who are we when we are not autonomous successes? We are the new creation made real in the Atonement. Therefore we can rejoice and not fret. In Christ we have peace and are blessed.

3. *Recovering a Deeper Understanding of Sin*

Allen C. McSween Jr.

The Loss of the Concept of Sin in Church and Culture

Once sin was a strong, foreboding word, with great power and drama. No other word in the English language articulated so powerfully the depths of the human dilemma. The concept of sin gave voice to the radical brokenness of life without falling into utter despair. It served to name the madness that keeps being played out in the headlines of every day's news without disillusionment or utopian fantasies.

But now, for a host of reasons, the stern old language of sin has fallen into disuse and disfavor. The word itself has a quaintness that smells of musty sanctuaries and renders its recovery problematic at best. Sin in our culture is more often used to name desserts and perfume than the depths of the human predicament. Mention the word sin at a cocktail party and listen to the embarrassed silence. Sin has become the ultimate conversation stopper, even in the church. Talk too much about sin in mainline Protestant churches and, one way or another, the congregation will let you know that they do not come to worship to be told "how bad they are." They come for enough uplift and encouragement to get them through another week. Sin-talk is such a "downer." It's bad for self-esteem, isn't it? The last thing in the world many of our members want from their religion is to make them or their children feel guilty.

In seeking to recover a deeper understanding of sin, we have work to do. Our task is not to attempt to outline "a biblical theology of sin," but to show how in Scripture sin is not described in the abstract or defined propositionally, but is rendered in "thickly textured" narratives that "read" us every bit as much as we read them.[16]

The Narration of Sin in Scripture

The biblical realism of sin is introduced in the story of human creation and crisis told in Genesis 2 and 3. There is debate about how much of the later Christian doctrine of sin can legitimately be found in the story. Rabbinic commentary on the passage does not treat it as the catastrophic "fall" portrayed in Roman Catholic or Protestant dogmatics. Walter Brueggemann says that even though "the text is commonly treated as the account of 'the fall,' nothing could be more remote from the narrative itself. . . . In general the Old Testament does not assume such a 'fall.'"[17] Neither is the story a narrative explanation of how evil entered the world. Such speculative matters were of little concern to the Old Testament writers. What is most significant for our purposes is the way in which the sin of Adam and Eve in all of its various aspects (disobedience, seeking to be like God, quest for autonomy) is portrayed essentially as a breach in their relationship to God with the resulting brokenness of all their other relationships to each other and the created order.

Interestingly enough, Brueggemann, perhaps more under the influence of neo-orthodoxy then than may be the case now, reads the story in typical Kierkegaardian fashion as a "theological critique of anxiety." Our anxiety comes from our mistaken pursuit of autonomous freedom, instead of accepting the limits and realities of our creaturehood from God.

In failing to "discern the boundaries of human life," we fall into an anxiety that in our culture we seek to resolve largely by "psychological, economic, cosmetic" means, all of which are bound to fail because they do not address the root cause of anxiety. Brueggemann notes that "Our public life is largely premised on an exploitation of our common anxiety. The advertising of consumerism and the drives of the acquisitive society, like the serpent, seduce us into believing there are securities apart from the reality of God."[18]

Whatever we make of our level of personal or social anxiety, it is surely right to locate sin in our pursuit of autonomous freedom, seeking to be our own arbiters of good and evil, and in our readiness to be seduced "into believing there are securities apart from the reality of God."

As a case in point, in the familiar story of David and Bathsheba (2 Samuel 11), we see the tragic results of David's pursuit of autonomous freedom expressed narratively in the repeated use of the sovereign word "send." The text offers a richly textured exploration of sin as it finds expression in the life of "a man after God's own heart." As is true throughout Scripture, sin is not defined. It is narrated in an artful narrative that reveals sin's insidious power in even the "best and brightest" — perhaps *especially* in the best and brightest.

Here, rather than comment on the story itself, I want to focus on the way the editors of the Psalms used the story of David's sin with Bathsheba as the narrative backdrop for Psalm 51, with its profound theological reflections on sin and repentance. Many features of the psalm suggest that it may have been composed during or after the exile. Its theology and language are closely related to those of Jeremiah, Ezekiel, and Isaiah 40-66. But the superscription above the psalm calls it "A psalm of David, when Nathan the prophet came to him, after he had gone in to Bathsheba." Thus the reader is invited to hear the psalm in the context of the "thick particularities" of the David story, even though its language for sin is quite general.

For the purposes of this paper the following points, suggested by James Mays in his excellent commentary on the Psalms, offer significant insights into the way sin is understood biblically.

a. The psalmist acknowledges his sin in the light of God's steadfast love and abundant mercy. He throws himself into the arms of the God he already knows to be gracious and merciful. The assurance of God's grace precedes the naming and confession of sin.

> The prayer is not merely an expression of human remorse or preoccupation with failure and guilt; it already looks beyond self to God and lays hold on the marvelous possibilities of God's grace. Confession of sin is already on the way to justification because it is first of all a response to grace.[19]

b. The psalmist knows that his sin is fundamentally against God and God alone. The idea that a person could sin without harming others would be inconceivable in the Old Testament. All sin obviously has social consequences. Yet properly understood, sin is essentially a theological concept.

> It is God and God alone whose way and will as criteria for human acts reveal them as sin. . . . It is the divine oversight of human life that makes talk about sin meaningful and necessary. Where there is no reckoning with the oversight of God, the vocabulary of sin becomes meaningless and atrophies.[20]

c. The psalmist confesses his own condition of sinfulness, not any particular sins. The terms used to confess the psalmist's guilt (sin, iniquity, transgression, blood-guiltiness, or violence) are general terms that do not confess specific transgressions "but a whole life conditioned by sin from its beginning." The psalmist confesses not just that

> I have sinned but that I am in my existence a sinner. My problem is not just the need of pardon for a particular wrong but deliverance from the predicament of my self. . . . Repentance concerns what I am, not just something I have done that is an expression of what I am. The confession of sin always has a corporate dimension.[21]

d. The confession of sin seeks renewal as well as forgiveness. The psalmist trusts the creative power of God's Holy Spirit to do that which he knows is utterly beyond his own power — to create in him a clean heart and renew a right (willing) spirit. The word "create" *(bārā')* is used exclusively in the Old Testament for that which God alone can do. The psalmist does not pray to be well adjusted to his sin. He does not ask for greater will-power to resist sin, or for a greater sense of self-esteem. He prays for a new creation at the center of his being. The psalmist confesses his sinfulness, not out of despair or self-pity, but in the assurance that out of honest contrition God will indeed re-create the human self from within.

We turn now briefly to Paul's wrestling with sin in his letter to the Romans. At first glance it might seem that the complex theological formulations of Romans are far removed from the narrative world of the Old Testament, but that is not the case. Reflections on Genesis 2–3 play a central role in Paul's development of sin, especially in his contrast between Adam and Christ. Both symbolize a narrative world that the Apostle assumes his readers know well.

Adam represents for Paul "the whole of humanity, fallen under the power of sin." In his commentary on Romans, Paul Achtemeier writes,

> The melancholy fact is . . . humans as a race repeat the sin of their original "ancestor." They seek to establish themselves as gods (Genesis 3:5). If then Adam is our "original" human, then his sin is the "original" sin, and those who belong to the race Adam began (all of us) fall under sin's power.[22]

For Paul, sin is essentially idolatry — worshiping the creature instead of the Creator, centering life around our own wants and desires instead of the gracious and life-giving will of the Creator. Achtemeier says that for Paul,

> The root of the human malaise, of human sin, is the substitution of something other than God the Creator and Father of Jesus Christ as Lord. It is the temptation to which Adam and Eve succumbed: the temptation to become God, and hence Lord, themselves, and it is, in Paul's view, the continuing root of our malaise.[23]

Theological Reflections on Sin

Let us move now to reflect theologically on the biblical narratives of sin. Sin in Scripture is narrated, not defined, because sin is not primarily the violation of a principle, a law, or a structure. It is the violation of an ongoing relationship with God, our Creator, Sustainer, and Redeemer. The Christian concept of sin makes no sense apart from God's eternal covenant to be with and for us in Jesus Christ.

However much we may lament the loss of the vocabulary of sin and evil in our culture, we must nevertheless insist that sin is a uniquely religious — indeed, theological — concept. Understood biblically, sin is not merely an ethical concept — something we *do* that is wrong. Sin is a *theological* concept — that which betrays or breaks our relationship with God. Fleming Rutledge is right: "Sin is only understood to be sin when God is understood to be God."[24] We only know sin in the light of God's will for our life together. Sin is not merely the violation of a moral code, however serious its consequences may be. Sin is the disruption of the relationship with God for which we were created by God. Its inevitable result is the disruption of all our relationships with nature, others, and our self.

The relationship for which God created us can best be understood in light of our intended vocation to "image God." Over the centuries there has been a great deal of debate about the meaning of the elusive phrase in Genesis, "image of God." Although relatively little is made of the phrase in the rest of Scripture, it has exercised a dominant influence in later reflections on theological anthropology. Our creation "in the image of God" has often been understood in terms of certain qualities we are said to possess by virtue of our creation — in particular, reason and freedom (self-transcendence). Following that line of thought, sin would best be understood as failing to live up to our high dignity and destiny as ones created in the very image of God. Such a view fits nicely into the Enlightenment view of human ascendancy, and finds expression in virtually all the "self-esteem" literature so popular in the church and in the culture today.

It seems to me, however, that it is far better to interpret the phrase "image of God" along lines suggested by John Calvin and nicely developed in our time by Douglas John Hall. In their view, the human creature is not so much made *in* the image of God as made to *image* God. The distinct human vocation is to reflect God's love in the world, to represent God's lordship in creation, to exercise responsible stewardship of the created order, "holding the world in trust for future generations of living things" (in the nice phrase from "A Declaration of Faith," PCUS) as the creature in whom creation finds its voice and lifts it in prayer. Hall writes,

> For Calvin the concept of the Imago Dei has already moved from the status of a noun to that of a verb. At base, what is referred to is not something that we *have* or *had* but something that we *do* or *fail to do.*

> We image God if and insofar as we are oriented toward God. Rightly turned to God, we reflect the divine image, as mirrors reflect what they are turned toward. The image of God is thus not a permanent endowment . . . but a quality that is dependent upon our posture vis-à-vis God.[25]

I find that approach very helpful. It keeps the focus on the relationship with God for which we were created and on the addressability by God that "makes and keeps human life human" (in Paul Lehmann's familiar phrase). To image God in the world means to be in a responsive relationship with the source and sustainer of all being and goodness. To refuse to live in that gracious relationship or to "miss the mark" of reflecting God's gracious lordship is sin. Daniel Migliori sums up well the implications of such a view:

> If being human in the image of God means life in free response to God who freely and graciously addresses us, then sin can be described as the denial of our relatedness to God and our need for God's grace. From this vantage point sin is fundamentally opposition to grace, saying No to the invitation to be human in grateful service to God and in fellowship with our fellow creatures. Sin is the great refusal to live thankfully and gladly by the grace of God that makes personal life in community with diverse others possible. Thus we misunderstand the depth of sin if we see it only as a violation of a moral code; it is, instead, primarily the disruption of our relationship to God.[26]

No writing on sin can close without a call to a more profound self-examination. We as Christians have a counter-witness to offer: *Mea culpa,* said neither in despair nor resignation but in profound trust in the Christ who "while we were yet sinners . . . died for us" (Romans 5:8). In that counter-witness, corporate worship has a vital role to play. Sermons on sin will likely fall on deaf ears in a culture saturated by the worship of self-esteem. But sermons that narrate sin honestly and forthrightly by staying close to the profound realism of Scripture can enable a congregation over a period of years to develop both the vocabulary and the theological imagination to reclaim the powerful vocabulary of sin.

4. Who Is the "I" In Psalm 51?

Albert H. Keller

No poem in the Book of Psalms is more spiritually and emotionally intense in its personal nature than Psalm 51. Who is this person standing before God, acutely conscious of sin and sin-sickness, praying for God to create a clean heart and to put a new and right spirit within? How does this person understand himself/herself? And how can we today understand this person before God? This prayer-psalm is frequently used when people of Christian and Jewish faith pray today. And so the question becomes how we understand ourselves, who make this prayer our own, the "I" who is the subject of the relation with God, or the "me" who is the object of God's action.

First Response: King David

The first reading is that proposed by the heading of the psalm itself: "A Psalm of David, when the prophet Nathan came to him, after he had gone in to Bathsheba." The "I" of the psalm is David at a precise moment in his personal narrative (II Samuel 11–12). Having seen and coveted Bathsheba, the king arranged a stratagem in which her husband Uriah would be killed. Now Uriah is dead and David has taken Bathsheba as his own wife, just as he desired, when he is visited by the prophet Nathan. We can imagine how David's heart must sink when he opens the door and there stands Nathan. The prophet tells the king a little story and it is a "mousetrap." David springs the trap and condemns himself as one deserving a punishment of death. It is only left for Nathan to pronounce the obvious. "You are the man." Exposed, incriminated by his own standard of justice, fully aware of the extent and depth of his covetousness and treachery, and also aware that he stands before the living God, the "I" who is David prays this absolutely truthful and grief-drenched prayer that is Psalm 51.

Wilhelm Vischer, Swiss Old Testament scholar, believed that the historical David, as profiled extensively in the narratives of Samuel, was himself the author of this psalm.[27] All we know about David — warrior, king, poet, musician, man of deep feeling and great soul — attests that he was capable of this expression. The existential event involving Uriah and Bathsheba, brought to a point of shocking significance by Nathan, was not only a momentous revelation to David of the extent of his self-deception and sin, however. It became also the ground for the theology of the second creation story, Genesis 2–3, that tells the story of humanity's original blessing and fall. It is plausible to argue that that narrative was composed by theologians of David's court. The language and theology of that narrative, in Vischer's estimation, are the same as the expression in Psalm 51. The spiritual perception of humanity's rebellion and alienation from God, a building block of Hebrew, Jewish, and Christian theology, may have been formulated out of the shock of self-recognition experienced by David at this very moment of existential truth.

On this reading, the "I" praying the psalm is the man David humbled by the power of self-recognition and judgment as a sinner before God. This reading satisfies a need to place a narrative in the personal context of an author whose life itself forms a narrative, as ours does, helping the reader to appropriate the written word personally. In this psalm, the sin is specific — David prays to be washed and cleansed from it — yet he also asks for a new, global act of creation in respect to his "heart" *(lēb)* and "spirit *(rûaḥ)*. Hans-Walter Wolff understands the prayer generally as one for the pure guidings of conscience plus the firm and steadfast will to act accordingly.[28] The resonances of David's treacherous act and profound repentance and grief make it much more than that for kindred souls.

Second Response: the Post-exilic Jewish Community

The second reading of this psalm places it in the context that current scholarship proposes as the psalm's most probable origin, based on its idiom and vocabulary as well as the final petition that God "rebuild the walls of Jerusalem; then you will delight in right sacrifices." That is the community of the exile and/or the post-exilic community in Jerusalem. By this time, the writings concerning David had become venerable and authoritative. David was viewed as the "prototypical case of the piety of dependence and trust represented by the psalms,"[29] much as Solomon became the patron and prototype of the wisdom expressed in Proverbs. This penitential prayer, prayed by a person who is in trouble and who identifies the cause of trouble uniquely as his/her sinful self, belongs to the Jewish community in both its liturgical usage and personal devotion. The amplitude of post-exilic Israel's penitence before God is both specified and intensified by the psalm's attachment to that well-known moment in the life of David.

In this context, the "I" of the psalm is both corporate and individual, as each member of the community of faith is integrated historically — with David and with each other — in response to God. Moreover, as the psalm belongs to the community, its form evolves as the community's usage changes, comparable to the way the language of classic hymns has changed to reflect the need for inclusiveness of the church community that uses them. In its present form, the psalm appears most resonant with the language and thought of Jeremiah, Ezekiel, and Isaiah 40–66. This is particularly true regarding the prayer that God create a clean heart and a new spirit (cf. Jeremiah 24:7, 31:33, 32:39-40; Ezekiel 36:25ff). The full theological concept of *bārā'* appears to have been formulated in this epoch of judgment and new creation — the historical and spiritual context also for the first creation story in Genesis 1.

In the psalm, the self and the community are integral in agency and responsibility, both heart and spirit being aspects of an integrated human being responding and accountable to the creative, life-giving spirit of God. The psalm cannot conceive the sinfulness of the human self without reference to God, because only before God do harmful actions become *sin.* Sin is theological: as verse 4 states, "against thee, thee only, have I sinned," echoing the confession of David when confronted by Nathan ("I have sinned against the Lord"). Action that harms other persons or the community is defined as *sin* because it is "that which is evil in thy sight." Nor can the sinful self be regarded without looking beyond the self to the grace of God, who creates anew. That is the understanding that resonates clearly with the prophets.

The definition of sin as being against God alone, in verse 4, is hyperbolic for emphasis. That vigorous expression is matched by the hyperbole of verse 5 with its reference to sinful conception and birth. (Note the suggestion of hyperbole also in verse 16.) Rather than detailing a belief in inherited sin or original sin as the "default position" of humanity, much less a notion that the sexual act of conception is itself sinful, this expression emphasizes the nature of sin as encompassing *the whole self fully extended in time* — back to conception. While a sinful act, such as David's, may be concrete and historical, "sin" is a condition that involves the whole self. There is no excusing oneself, no pleas of temporary insanity or "the devil made me do it," in response to God. (Both Isaiah and Ezekiel also expressed the sin of Israel as going back to the very beginning — cf. Isaiah 50:1). That is why a new divine act of creation *(bārā')* of a new *lēb* and the "renewal" of a steadfast *rûaḥ* are necessary. A radical problem requires a radical solution.

To summarize, the "I" of Psalm 51, as used liturgically and devotionally by the dynamic community of the exile and beyond, understands an integrative self or *lēb* that is fully tainted by sin and absolutely in need of purification, because the whole self lives before God. One thinks of Paul's hyperbolic expression of the same truth: "I am the chief of sinners." If God withdrew God's spirit in response to this uncleanness (verse 11), one could not live. Therefore the "I" requires and prays for an act of new creation, in which a clean heart (one open to God) and a steady spirit renew selfhood. This renewal is clearly an act of grace. Moreover, the insistence of the prayer that sin is not episodic but holistic strongly suggests that the new creation is not seen as a one-off event in one historical moment, but a continual creating of a heart that is in quality broken and contrite, and a constant renewing of a spirit that is steady in its correspondence with the divine spirit of life. The "I" may be individual and it may be corporate, and it may be both at once, for both aspects of Israel live before God's judgment and grace.

Third Response: Christian and Church — The Person and Community in Christ

The profound spiritual moves made by the one who prays Psalm 51 call out for incarnation. Human experience alone, then or now, within the faith community or outside, does not validate either the absolute need for purification or the realization of new creation.

In the person of Jesus of Nazareth, the Church affirms in its canonical scriptures, the mediator appears. Jesus' communion with God brings holiness to earth, sharply defining both sin and transformation; Jesus' crucifixion and resurrection signal to believers the full extent of sin and the reality of new creation. As Paul formulated the theological dynamics, the humanly insurmountable double bind of sin (Romans 7) is resolved in the grace of God fully revealed in Christ, who was made to be sin though he knew no sin, so that in him we might become the righteousness of God. The new creation is accomplished, in Paul's (and the Church's) understanding, when we are able by faith to say, "I, yet not I, but Christ who lives in me."

The "I" of Psalm 51, therefore, as prayed by the Church, is Christ first, in whom both the sin and the renewal/new creation are realized, and myself second, as one who lives by the faith of the Son of God. In Christ, the *rûaḥ* is not withdrawn from me but promised and present. As I pray Psalm 51, it becomes not a desperate plea but a soul-deepening rehearsal of the terms of my relationship with God. It is truth that is being accomplished and fulfilled, as the new creation constantly happens in response to the living God. As my spirit is sustained and made willing by the Holy Spirit, then I join God's creation as I teach transgressors God's ways, and other sinners turn. The psalm is mine because I am Christ's, and I trust that it is being realized even as I pray it.

Fourth Response: Theological Anthropology in the Context of Evolutionary Biology

Shaped thoroughly by Paul and his profound understanding of God's relationship with humanity (Israel and the gentiles) through spiritual union with the crucified and risen Christ, the Church's anthropology must now be shaped also by a critical coherence with a scientific understanding of humanity as part of created nature.

That is to say: the "I" of Psalm 51 is a person/Church in Christ; but that same "I" is also evolutionary, historical/cultural, and emergent (open, not determined). That "I" is relational and interdependent with other humans, the community of life, and the web of nature; non-hierarchical but part of a whole ecological system; multi-leveled in terms of systems of explanation; capable of love, freedom, moral responsibility, growth/novelty, joy in beauty, suffering, and spiritual experience.

Operationally, then, the fourth response to the question of who is the "I" of Psalm 51 must incorporate (to the extent any of us is capable of critically using them) the scientific disciplines that study human beings, such as neurobiology, evolutionary psychology, human behavioral ecology, human development, anthropology, and the sciences of complexity and chaos in relation to human affairs. Although I am incapable of such a synthesis, I hopefully affirm that a theological anthropology for the twenty-first century must take these disciplines into full account as partners in dialogue. Theology is changing in response to new human understandings of ourselves as part of that deep and complex process we call the created universe.

A core hypothesis concerning the "I" of Psalm 51, then, may be stated as follows: The human being is created by God, by means of the long processes of natural evolution and spiritual intervention, to be God's co-creator, acting in freedom as both architect and builder in the continuing creation that God has brought into being and for which God has purposes. This core hypothesis is heavily indebted to theologian Philip Hefner.[30] Using a methodology proposed by Imre Lakatos for research programs in science and applicable to other disciplines, Hefner articulates the heart of his system, his *core hypothesis,* as unprovable (because it cannot be falsified) yet plausible, robust, and grounded in the experience of faith and reason. Surrounding and buffering his core hypothesis, Hefner proposes "auxiliary" hypotheses that expand on the core and bind it to the world of empirical, verifiable experience. Christian faith is fundamentally a message about the world, Hefner asserts; therefore theology cannot do its work unless it integrates within its procedures the disciplines of thought necessary to gain knowledge about the world, such as the natural and anthropological sciences.

To expand on my core hypothesis above, the human being has emerged from within the natural evolutionary processes as a creation who can scan its world, collect data, and construct complex interpretations of its experience in the world. Moreover, this creature has adapted so successfully to its global ecosystem that it has been able to impose an overlay upon the nonhuman systems of nature. Those systems are thoroughly conditioned now by human cultural inputs. This means that the further evolution of the biosphere is essentially connected to the evolved human being, who through his/her culture continually seeks to bring his/her genes and the rest of the environment into conditions of existence that only the culture-creating co-creator of the world would ever dream of. And finally, to this naturalistic account of the identity of the human being in the world we bring the basic faith assertion of Psalm 51: human beings stand fully accountable to God, whose spirit calls them into being and gives them life.

The crucial question imposed by the Psalm is this: how does *sin/penitence* function in a scientific context of evolutionary process?

That question calls for auxiliary hypotheses to respond. Hefner does not move in this direction — he is very helpful in exploring the evolutionary matrix of human development and what is meant by human freedom, but he does not deal with what people of faith have understood as sin. This may be a common stumbling block for process thinkers. Freedom, as conceptualized in this theory, comprises self-awareness, decision, action, and responsibility.[31] But what of the consciousness of the "I" praying Psalm 51, "against thee, thee only, have I sinned . . ."?

The first auxiliary hypothesis could be stated as follows: In freedom, the human being breaks the collegial relationship with the Creator by pursuing selfish purposes that forfeit the life-sustaining purpose of God. This leads to death (i.e., "un-creation"). The prayer of the 51st Psalm drives the second auxiliary hypothesis: In the remedial creative act of God mediated by the incarnation, death and resurrection of Jesus Christ, and by the sustained presence of the risen Christ in the world that the Church calls Holy Spirit, the human function of *created co-creator* is restored; God's purpose is revealed, chosen, and followed and humans are sustained by the Spirit when they pursue it.

A third auxiliary hypothesis is needed to qualify and expand the second and to amplify the creation theology of the core: The purpose of God that orders continuing creation can be perceived and pursued when humanity assiduously brings human knowledge in the physical and human sciences, arts, and humanities, into critical dialogue with that full vision of *shalom* prophesied in the Hebrew scriptures and lived and taught by Jesus.

Conclusion

Paul spoke of bringing every thought into captivity to Christ — meaning, I believe, that the touchstone of truth in all human knowledge and wisdom is the fully understood person of Christ. Human knowledge, if not wisdom, is not only vastly different from the body of knowledge in Paul's time; it is now exponentially increasing such that the quantity of knowledge (or information) doubles approximately every four to five years, and it is predicted that by the year 2025 it may double every seventy days. The short catalogue of sciences relevant to the study of human nature, cited earlier in this essay, is part of this information explosion. The sciences that contribute to our understanding of ecology are equally pertinent to the "religious enterprise" of sharing responsibly in the work of creation. Knowledge of a different kind, generated by artists and those who interpret texts, is an essential part of the mix.

Alone, however, the sciences and humanities cannot find direction in consonance with the purpose of God — they cannot create myth and ritual truthful enough, compelling enough, to construct the reality that can bring us steadily through this perilous epoch. Therein lies the aspiration of Paul, which he expressed as bringing all human culture "into captivity to Christ." He modeled in his apostolate to the gentiles, particularly those enculturated in Hellenistic and Latin ways, a kind of *asymmetrical integration* of the Christ meaningful in a Hebrew-Jewish frame with the concepts and philosophies of the gentiles. His risky venture affirmed his conviction that Christ is Lord of all.

Is the *myth* of which Psalm 51 is expressive transformed and intensified when spoken in a Christian voice adequate to the task of grounding the religious enterprise in the twenty-first century? The calling of the Church is to manifest that myth as spiritual and historical reality, indeed the true reality that alone can sustain wholesome life and assure the future. Insofar as we do so, we are becoming who we are created to be, cocreators with God of the world and all that is in it, responsive and responsible, until Christ who is the principle of all things becomes all in all.

CHAPTER II

The Person in Christian Tradition

Introduction

A global civilization is rapidly developing throughout many parts of the developed world through the rapid growth of sophisticated forms of transportation, mass media, and industrial and biomedical technology. Concurrently, however, we are also in the throes of regional wars, "ethnic cleansings," and fundamentalist, sectarian violence and terrorism, all conspicuously allied with competing theological ideologies. Advocates of the former are often motivated by a secular humanism that rejects some of the essential tenets of coexisting religions throughout the world. Proponents of the latter are tempted to claim an exclusive hold on the revelation of God (or truth) that can lead to the destructive demonization of the threatening "others." Clearly there is a pressing need for all to find and practice more theologically acceptable ways of validating mutual accommodation, civil toleration, and critical respect and cooperation among different groups of persons on our "shrinking" planet. What are some helpful insights and resources in the Christian anthropological tradition?

W. Rush Otey challenges current American forms of Pelagian humanism by recalling their orthodox repudiation by Augustine and ecumenical councils of the ancient church. Intending to improve the everyday lives of his peers, Pelagius advocated a rigorous and virtuous lifestyle. He denied original sin and affirmed human free will for knowing and doing the saving good in following Christ's moral teaching and example. Thereby he allegedly championed an optimistic anthropology that encouraged righteousness by human works. In strong opposition, Augustine centered on the biblical message of human salvation and service through the redemptive power of God's grace embodied in the life, death, and resurrection of Jesus Christ. To offset their solidarity in original sin, humans were in need of God's prevenient grace in baptism, and growth in sanctifying grace through sacramental participation in the saving and serving mission of Christ's church.

John Christopherson stresses that anthropology is indispensable for ethical decision-making. This is especially true for the myriad of new challenges in such current biomedical issues as abortion, euthanasia, genetic engineering, transplants, cloning, and stem-cell harvesting. Competing anthropological hypotheses emerge from rationalist, empirical, idealistic, and pragmatic perspectives, and sources of sexual research. A theological view that understands the human in primary relation to God must be added to this cultural mix in a pluralistic society. John Calvin declared that "knowledge of ourselves and knowledge of God are correlative." A central category of debate is the "image of God," both in the Genesis creation narrative and in the New Testament praise of the Christ whose mystery "holds all things together" (Colossians 1:17).

Joseph A. Bassett provides a concrete pastoral care illustration of the pertinence of Christian anthropology to modern biomedical hospital practice. He serves as a community representative in advising hospital administrators regarding the advisability of clinical research proposals submitted to an Institutional Review Board by different departments of the hospital. Risk/benefit issues tend to dominate the discussions today, but the Christian pastor has a distinctive contribution to make in representing theological views that allegedly have universal applicability. For example, both Roman Catholic and Reformed ecumenical studies have grounded statements regarding human rights and abortion in the biblical witness to the image of God. Pertinent sections may be located in the Genesis creation saga, and in the New Testament witness to Jesus Christ and to those baptized believers who enjoy a new nature through faith in Christ. The author holds that in his life, death, and resurrection, Christ reveals the image of the invisible God whose hidden will is the basis of universal human rights.

5. *The New Pelagians*

W. Rush Otey

Revisiting the early-fifth-century controversy between the British theologian and reformer Pelagius and Augustine, Bishop of Hippo, provides insights and guidance through many of the weaknesses and controversies in the contemporary Church. Modern forms of Pelagian thought and practice both weaken the witness of the Church and threaten to divide the Body of Christ.

Pelagius' Understanding of Human Nature

Pelagius was a devout and sincere Christian, possibly a monk or at least a teacher of theology. He was of Celtic origins. In the year 400 he came to Rome and was appalled by the low morals and lax practices of the Church and society. To his credit he set about to provide a prophetic word of exhortation in order to improve the religious and ethical lives of his peers.

For Pelagius, much of the problem resulted from a misunderstanding of grace and from a doctrine of human nature that expected too little from people. As John Leith has put it, "Pelagius had a great vision of human dignity and of the power of the human self to determine its own life, and he had a great vision of what it means to be a Christian individually and socially. Many of the homeless, confused people of the time, who had sensed that life should be better than it was, were attracted to Pelagius, and under his influence many lives were transformed."[1]

Pelagius wrote from the mainstream traditions of the faith. He quoted widely from Lactantius, Hilary of Poitiers, Ambrose, John Chrysostom, Jerome, and Augustine himself. His commentary on the epistles of Paul was widely respected. He was no wild-eyed individualist who set out to plot his own course. Pelagius sought to be an apologist for orthodoxy, in part motivated to refute the dualistic anthropology found in Manichaeism (which Augustine had earlier embraced) and Marcionism.

Pelagius believed that human beings originally are endowed by the Creator with a rational will (this is his understanding of the *"imago Dei"*).

By using this gift, people can ascend in moral virtue and even be without sin. The law of Moses was given in order to strip humanity of its ignorance of the right use of the will, and to serve as a guide to overcome sin and bad habits. God further showed grace in giving Jesus as an example; the teachings of Jesus are to be considered divine law to be followed, as well as rational truths concerning the proper relationship of human beings to God and to each other.[2]

Pelagius observed that the thoroughgoing emphasis of Augustine and others that even the capacity to believe, have faith, and follow Jesus is an undeserved and free gift resulted in too much passivity and even sloth. The gift for Pelagius was to be discovered in the human ability to become, to do better. Sin, for Pelagius, was the failure to do what law and reason could indeed reveal and attain; sin is slackness, and its antidote is effort, concentration, and desire to overcome bad habits. A well-known sentence of Pelagius comes from a letter to Demetrias upon her taking vows to become a holy virgin in the year 413: "Since perfection is possible for man, it is obligatory."[3]

Pelagius held that human beings are not born sinful creatures; God is Creator, and God, being perfectly good, cannot create sin. In this affirmation, Pelagius denied the concept of original sin and also the dualistic concept of the eternal divide between flesh and spirit. Adam's fall therefore affected only Adam. There is no transmission of sin by procreation. The fall of Adam affected humanity — grievously to be sure — in that it provided the example of sin for Adam's offspring and began the human misuse of the rational free will endowed by the Creator. The presence of sin in the world is due to humanity's lack of education, to their making bad choices and falling into bad habits, to following Adam's bad examples and after a time setting even poorer examples.

It is therefore possible for some people in Scripture (Abel, Melchizedek, Abraham, Job, Jesus) and in the present to be without sin; these people employed their free will and were reckoned righteous by God. Most people, however, remain enslaved to their habits and their erroneous choices. For Pelagius, the concept of freedom of the will was crucial for there to be any meaningful talk about virtue, since true virtue implies the decision for good and against evil. What virtue can there be in a person who has no choice but to behave as he or she does?

The fact that people have free wills does not place them outside the sovereignty of God, since free will is the bestowal of God. Pelagius enumerates three foundations of human freedom: (1) *"posse,"* or ability or possibility, which in its pure form can be properly ascribed only to God who alone confers it upon His creatures; (2) *"velle,"* or will/volition; (3) *"esse,"* or existence/actuality. *Velle* and *esse* have their source in the human being, but there can be no *velle* or *esse* without the *posse* of God. Again the letter to Demetrias is revealing: "No one knows the extent of our strength better than He who gave us that strength. . . . He has not willed to command anything which is impossible, for He is righteous; and He will not condemn a man for what he could not help, for He is holy."[4]

Over the course of his writings, then, Pelagius holds that people are more able than they appear to be. God in His justice did not lay upon the Jews any moral requirements that were impossible to fulfill. A God who is truly good would not order people to do the impossible and then damn them for not being able to keep these impossible commandments. Christ said, "Be ye perfect," and this implies the real possibility of obedience to perfection. Further, if people "cannot" be without sin, it is not fair to attach guilt to them, and the Bible is full of passages concerning the guilt of humanity. The death of Christ as a historical occasion allows for the past sins of humanity to be forgiven; Christ's teaching and perfect example open up the possibility of sinless life via the "narrow gate." The Holy Spirit is God's further gracious provision of a guide and of the necessary "illumination" by which human beings are aided in their striving.

What Pelagius conceives is not a state of perfection or bliss acquired once and for all time, but rather one attained by strenuous efforts, which only steadily increasing application will be able to maintain. It is thus a state only attainable by the converted person. As Pelagius affirmed before the second synod of Palestine in 415, "No one is able to be without sin unless he has acquired knowledge of the law. The beginning of obedience is the will to know what is commanded." Apart from God, people cannot achieve perfection; with God, all things are possible.

Faith, for Pelagius, is not the mere adherence to rules but is "trust from the whole heart." Baptism is the sacrament of justification by faith alone; for adults baptism is regenerative and medicinal. For infants, baptism is benedictory, since they have no sin until they misuse their wills.

Peter Brown, an eminent biographer of Augustine, describes what was at stake for Pelagius in the "culture wars" of his day:

> Pelagianism had appealed to a universal theme: the need of the individual to define himself, and to feel free to create his own values in the midst of the conventional, second-rate life of society. In Rome, the weight of convention was particularly oppressive. The families, whose members Pelagius addressed, had lapsed gradually into Christianity by mixed marriages and politic conformity. This meant that the conventional "good man" of pagan Rome had quite unthinkingly become the conventional "good Christian" of the fifth century. The flamboyant courtesies of Late Roman etiquette could pass as "Christian humility" and the generosity traditionally expected of an aristocrat as "Christian alms-giving." "It is better to give than to receive" was a popular tag; but, like all Biblical citations used to ease the conscience, no one could quite remember where it came from! Yet these "good Christians," "true believers," were still members of a ruling class committed to maintaining the Imperial laws by administering brutal punishments. They were prepared to fight tooth and nail to protect their vast properties, and were capable of discussing at the dinner table both the latest theological opinion, on which they had prided themselves as experts, and the kind of judicial torture they had just inflicted on some poor wretch.
>
> In this confusion, the harsh, firm message of Pelagius came as a deliverance. He would offer the individual absolute certainty through absolute obedience.[5]

And yet . . . Augustine's Anthropology

Augustine and Pelagius apparently never met face to face. Their theological debate was carried on either through letters or through their friends. In 412 Coelestius, a disciple of Pelagius, was challenged for his views on original sin and baptism by a synod at Carthage. His views were refuted. Pelagius was confronted by two synods in Palestine in 415, but was acquitted, much to the dismay of Jerome and Augustine. Another council was held in Carthage in 418, at which Pelagius' theology was condemned. At the third ecumenical council of the church in Ephesus in 431, Pelagius was anathematized. Jaroslav Pelikan and others have observed that the Pelagian-Augustinian debates in the councils of the Church may be viewed as the extension of the rivalry between the Eastern and Western theological factions dating back to the time of Origen. Indeed, the most explicit statement made about Pelagius by an exclusively Eastern synod (the second synod in Palestine in 415) was the acknowledgment that "he belongs to the communion of the Catholic Church."[6]

Though in some instances the two were in concert, the differences between Augustine and Pelagius were significant and finally incompatible. As R. C. Sproul put it, "(Pelagianism) removes the 'sola' from 'sola gratia' and ultimately the 'sola' from 'sola fide.'"[7]

Augustine differed from Pelagius with regard to understanding Creation, fall, human captivity to sin, and the necessity of grace through Christ's death and resurrection — a necessity not mitigated by good intentions or more diligent efforts. For Augustine, the image of God is not so much in the original rectitude and capacity of human rationality but in the restlessness of the human heart to be with God; but this restlessness itself is the work not of the will but of the gift and the presence of the Creator/Spirit:

> If anyone contends that in any age human nature did not stand in need of the second Adam as its physician, on the ground that it was not corrupted in the first Adam, he is shown up as an enemy of the grace of Christ, being in error not in respect of some questions where uncertainty or error is possible without detriment to the faith, but in respect of the rule of faith itself, which is the basis of our Christianity. . . . They do not observe that humanity was then sunk in such grievous and intolerable sins that by a just judgment of God the whole world was wiped out by a flood, save for one man of God, and his wife, and their three sons and their wives. . . . Thus, from the moment when through one man sin came into the world, and death through sin, and thus passed to all mankind, since all sinned in him, the whole mass of perdition became the possession of the destroyer. So that no one, no one at all, has been set free from that situation, or is being set free, or will be set free, except by the grace of the Redeemer.[8]

For Augustine, a human being can no more choose to save or even improve himself or herself than an empty glass can fill itself. While agreeing with Pelagius that human beings still have wills and can make choices, he observed that people have lost their moral liberty because the desires are chained by their own limited and complex commitment and insights. For human beings it is impossible not to sin. "In saying this," he wrote, "we are not doing away with free will. For who could benefit except one who willed in humility, not pluming himself on the strength of his will, as if that alone sufficed for perfect righteousness?[9] . . . God produces in man the will to believe, and in everything 'his mercy goes before us.'"[10]

Augustine steadfastly held that in the final analysis, Pelagius reduced the Incarnation to an edifying example of what could happen for each person, and obscured the necessity of the Cross for redemption and the power of the Resurrection for the human future. Thus, Augustine is at once more Christocentric and Trinitarian. Despite human sin and frailty, the good news is in Christ alone and not in moral attainments, in the gift of the Redeemer and not in the Creation:

> The Son of God assumed human nature, and in it he endured all that belongs to the human condition. This is a remedy for mankind of a power beyond human imagining. Could any pride be cured, if the humility of God's Son does not cure it? Could any greed be cured, if the poverty of God's Son does not cure it? Or any coldness, if the love of God's Son does not cure it? Lastly, what fearfulness can be cured, if it is not cured by the resurrection of the body of Christ the Lord? Let mankind raise its hopes, and recognize its own nature; let it observe how high a place it has in the works of God. Do not despise yourselves, you men; the Son of God assumed manhood. Do not despise yourselves, you women; God's Son was born of a woman. But do not set your hearts on the satisfactions of the body, for in the Son of God we are "neither male or female." Do not set your heart on temporal rewards; if it were good to do so, that human nature which God's Son assumed would have thus set its heart. Do not fear insults, crosses, and death; for if they did man harm, the humanity which God's Son assumed would not have endured them.[11]

Though unintentionally, the Pelagians, because of their high anthropology, veered toward an impossible legalism (all the while urging "possibility"!), and toward asceticism, and toward a theology close to deism. Augustine, a more realistic observer of human behaviors and history, and a more subtle interpreter of Scripture, saw that only by incarnate grace and prevenient mercy can a human being endure, let alone enter into everlasting life. It could be argued that for Augustine, grace was not simply part of Christian theology, not one doctrine or idea among many; grace is in a sense the only thing that matters:

> The grace of God through Jesus Christ our Lord must be understood as that by which alone men are delivered from evil, and without which they do absolutely no good thing, whether in thought, or will and affection, or in deed; not only in order that they may know by the manifestation of the same what should be done, but moreover in order that by its enabling they may do with love what they know.[12]

Comtemporary Challenges

Were it not so popular in Robert Schuller's instance, Pelagianism could well be reduced to caricature. It was also popular in the fifth century — else Augustine would not have wasted his energy. Much is at stake in the consideration of nature and grace, of fall and redemption. Throughout the history of the United States, Pelagius is often regnant through such means as Ben Franklin's aphorisms, Emerson's "Self-Reliance," and the revivalism that insists upon prescribed actions and a willed decision to insure salvation — to say nothing of self-help movements both religious and non-religious. How often does one hear sincere sentiments such as, "It really doesn't matter what a person believes as long as he/she follows the Golden Rule. . . . I am an ethical and spiritual person but not into religion or worship. . . . Is it the Truth? Is it Fair to all concerned? Will it build Good Will and Better Friendships? Will it be Beneficial to all concerned?" (The Rotary International Four-Way Test).

I struggle with the Pelagian temptation in my own life and ministry — in my stewardship sermons, in my attempt to relate the congregation I serve to our local environmental disasters, in my difficulty in letting go of my lamenting of choices I did not make that I should have made, in my insomniac distresses, in pastoral care ("He's got to hit bottom and decide to work on it before I can be any help to him"), and in the innumerable yet surmountable ingratitudes of a censorious posture toward the other people I know and don't like.

But Augustine is by far the more difficult and exacting mentor. Grace is tougher and more perplexing than law, trust more risky than certitude, and admitting one's own sin less appealing than "getting oneself together" or "marching as to war." Here, then, is offered a theology founded upon the authority of Scripture, adhering to the death of the Messiah, living in the promise of the eschaton, and confessing that until then, "nothing in all creation shall ever separate us from the love of God in Christ Jesus our Lord" (Romans 8:35). Not even our well-intentioned, ethically vigorous, stupid choices shall separate us.

6. The Human: Its Import for Ethical Decision-Making

John Christopherson

Introduction

Quaestio mihi factus sum ("A question I have become to myself")[13] — this ponderous line from St. Augustine's *Confessions*[14] sets the general grounding question for this investigation of the *humanum* from various perspectives and their respective import for biomedical ethics. What is the human being? This question is at once probably the most difficult to answer and yet one of the most important to be asked.[15] With the exception of the recent Human Genome Project, it could well be argued that we have been much more diligent in studying the non-human environment than in studying ourselves.

Many would probably consider this question of "What does it mean to be a human being?" to be overly obtuse or theoretical, especially in pragmatic America. However, when the question is reformulated or reversed as "What is being human?" or "What is the human thing to do?" then the matter of its radical relevancy becomes most apparent, especially in the fairly new field of biomedical ethics. In *Christian Anthropology and Ethics,* James M. Childs states that "Anthropology and ethics belong together."[16] Thus, one might contend that the matter of seeking to do the human(e) act raises the question of what it means to be a human being.[17] And so the question that finally prevails upon us is this: "Are we really clear on what we mean, or what the referent is, when we speak about the human being or human person in relation to something being either a humanizing or a dehumanizing act?"[18]

The word "human" is heard and read in daily events more and more frequently. It is broadly used as if its meaning were clear, its reference universally understood, and its persuasiveness unexceptionable. This can be illustrated, for example, by the frustration one experiences in seeking a normative definition of what it means to be "human" in the dictionary. In *Webster's New Collegiate Dictionary,* looking under "human," one reads, "of, or relating to or characteristic of man." Or again, when looking under "human nature," one reads, "the nature of man." Moreover, the rhetoric of Paul Ramsey's *Fabricated Man* that "We should not play God before we have learned to be [human beings]"[19] might be fine for a Sunday morning sermon, but it leaves unanswered any significant attempt at unpacking what it means to be human beings — at least with any precision. And who would accept the serial killer's plea, perhaps one who is even able to quote Pelagius: "We are *only human,* our flesh is weak!"[20] In the news we read about abortion clinic bombings by individuals who perform such violent acts — often injuring innocent bystanders — "for the sake of the human voices who cannot speak" (i.e. the unborn fetuses).[21] Suffice it to say that "Who or what is the human being?" is not self-evident or able to be grounded in intuition alone.

Understanding the *Humanum:* Its Relation to Biomedical Ethics

Probably more than any other enterprise, biomedical ethics has served to raise our consciousness to realize the ever-increasing importance of what is at stake when we speak of the human being. Buried deep within this whole field — involving issues of euthanasia, abortion, genetic engineering, transplants, and stem-cell harvesting — is this ubiquitous question: "What is it that makes the human being human? What is human about the human being?"

> This question underlies the whole range of medical issues today. . . . The question hovers over the dying process; when are we prolonging a biological existence which has ceased to be meaningful and recogniz-

> ably human? The question is ever present in the abortion issue: when are we dealing with a bit of tissue, and when are we dealing with a human being in the uterus? The question pervades the area of genetic control, of transplant surgery, of sex-change operations, and a host of others: when are we promoting authentically human existence?[22]

By now, it should be apparent that the concern for what it means to be a human being is a presuppositional question that necessitates an answer — not only for given acts in general, but specifically for decision-making in biomedical ethics. This concern for what it means to be human in various medical decision-making settings is evidenced by such recent titles as *The Patient as Person,*[23] *Human Medicine,*[24] *Human Existence — Medicine and Ethics,*[25] *Humanhood: Essays in Biomedical Ethics,*[26] *Human Cloning: Religious Responses,*[27] and *Playing God? Genetic Determinism and Human Freedom.*[28]

The obstacles to developing a consensus on what constitutes the normatively human appear to be insuperable. And certainly the expectation that all people in all cultures could ever agree upon some given list is rather utopian. Different cultures have different conceptions of human rights and values, and therefore the fact of cultural relativism prohibits the achievement of a perfect consensus. Moreover, at different stages of this development, people and their respective cultures have different norms related to the particular problems they are currently addressing.[29] This has become most evident in our age of increasing pluralism. But are we then to give up on attempting a normative definition of what it means to be human? Abraham Heschel offers this response:

> Just as death is the liquidation of being, dehumanization is the liquidation of being human. What qualifies a being to be called a human being? No one definition can fathom the depth of human being, the intricate ways and byways in whom it is disclosed. Yet to claim that the question is unanswerable, and the problem is insoluble, would be to surrender the hope of any knowledge concerning significant issues, since the question and the significance of all other questions we ask depends upon the answer we are ready to offer to this one.[30]

Certainly any effort to move toward even a modest consensus of what it means to be human must face certain basic epistemological issues. How does one come to know what is normatively human? What warrants can be given for any attempted normative definition of what it means to be human? How are human rights and values to be known? What constitutes the human in a human being?

7. Christian Anthropology in a Hospital Committee

Joseph A. Bassett

In medical centers, committees on clinical research are mandated to have members of the community among their number. Not infrequently one of these persons is a Christian minister. Along with everyone else, the minister receives a packet of research proposals from the various departments of the hospital: infectious disease, oncology, hematology, cardiology, adolescent medicine, or psychiatry. Every protocol is read and reviewed by two members of the committee sometimes known as an IRB, Institutional Review Board. At the meeting of the full committee, the various reviewers present their comments and recommendations.

First, there is a paraphrase of what is being proposed as well as what is involved. Reviewers want to be sure that the procedures involved are clearly explained. They may suggest a word change here and there or a few added sentences to make the procedure clearer to the patient.

The committee will calculate the risks and benefits involved. Hopefully, benefits outweigh risks. But how is that determined? The probability and magnitude of harm is considered over against any anticipated benefits. Usually, at this point the decision is made whether or not to let the research proceed. But every now and again that doesn't happen.

When a truly difficult issue arises in these protocols, there is a distinct shift of tone. A silence emerges when the calculus of risk versus benefit doesn't look promising. The silence deepens as reviewers speak more carefully. As the chairperson touches on the troubling issues, members of the committee grow pensive.

Pediatric AIDS Protocol 076 is a good example. It asked whether a dose of AZT *et al.* given to an HIV-infected mother at delivery would block the transmission of HIV to her newborn. Does AZT block the transmission of HIV in newborns or not? In 1993 no one knew which was true. Without the protocol, all that could be said was that seven out of ten such children would in all probability throw off the HIV infection some weeks after birth. Three would not. The choice before the committee was, Do you subject seven newborns to a dose of toxic drugs for the sake of the three who might remain infected? There was no benefit and perhaps harm to the seven no matter what the result for the three. To do the Protocol or not? Silence after intense questions.

At the heart of the decision on protocols like this is the way those sitting around the table understand the humanity of the women and children to be enrolled in the research protocols. When the committee members voice the reasons for their votes, decidedly different anthropologies come into play. At that point, a Christian minister may very well recognize a parting of the ways. How many of the assembled doctors, surgeons or psychiatrists, how many of the social workers or nurses, how many of the educators think of the men, women, and children who come to a teaching hospital as having been created in the image of God? The anthropology of perhaps one or two members of the committee (beside the minister) will be informed by the *imago.*

Even so, there will be a difference of opinion among those two or three members, since the "image of God" has more than one context in Scripture. When considering a protocol like 076, it does make a difference which one of these Christian committee members take up. In Round III of the Roman Catholic/Presbyterian-Reformed Consultation from 1976-79, the Consultation published two statements in 1980 under the title *Ethics and the Search for Christian Unity.*[31] "A Statement on Abortion" and "A Statement of Human Rights" make up the text. The two statements are enhanced by the Roman Catholic and Reformed commentary accompanying each of the statements.

Both statements, the one on human rights and the one on abortion, cite "the image of God." The Reformed commentary to "A Statement on Human Rights" notes the image of God in creation, Christ, and the Christian person.[32] Each of these contexts has a particular accent and evokes definite implications.

The first setting for the image of God is in the creation saga of the Hebrew Scriptures:

> Then God said, "Let us make man in our image, after our likeness; and let them have dominion over the fish of the sea, and over the birds of the air, and over the cattle and over all the earth, and over every creeping thing that creeps upon the earth." So God made man in his own image, in the image of God created he them; male and female he created them. (Genesis 1:26-27)

> This is the book of the generations of Adam. When God created man, he made him in the likeness of God. (Genesis 5:1)

> Whoever sheds the blood of man, by man shall his blood be shed; for God made man in his own image. (Genesis 9:6)

There are references found in the New Testament to the image of God in terms of the creation. Some have been suppressed. Others are simply unfamiliar.

> For a man ought not to cover his head, since he is the image and glory of God, but woman is the glory of man. (1 Corinthians 11:7)

> With it (the tongue) we bless the Lord and Father, and with it we curse men, who are made in the likeness of God. (James 3:9)

The second cluster of Biblical references to the image of God involves Jesus Christ. The Reformed commentary cites

> In their case the god of this world has blinded the minds of the unbelievers to keep them from seeing the light of the gospel of the glory of Christ, who is the likeness of God. (2 Corinthians 4:4)

> He is the image of the invisible God, the first-born of all creation; for in him all things were created, in heaven and earth, visible and invisible, whether thrones or dominions or principalities or authorities — all things were created through him and for him. (Colossians 1:15)

The third cluster of images refers to the new nature a person has in Christ. The commentary cites four texts from the epistles:

> And all of us, with unveiled faces, seeing the glory of the Lord, as though reflected in a mirror, are being transformed into the same image from one degree of glory to another. . . . (2 Corinthians 3:18)

> . . . seeing that you have put off the old nature with its practices and have put on the new nature which is being renewed in knowledge after the image of its creator. (Ephesians 4:24)

> Put off your old nature, which belongs to your former manner of life and is corrupt through deceitful lusts, and be renewed in the spirit of your minds, and put on the new nature, created after the likeness of God in true righteousness and holiness. (Colossians 3:9-10)

> Just as we have borne the image of the man of dust, we will also bear the image of the man of heaven. (1 Corinthians 15:49)

Understanding these texts in the tradition of pastors and theologians accentuates significant elements of a Christian anthropology. A text from each of these clusters with comments of venerable pastor-theologians helps the Christian minister to understand the women and children in Protocol 076. So what does an anthropology based on the image of God in creation, Christ, and humanity bring to the table of an ethics committee reviewing research protocols like 076? A Christian anthropology so informed alerts the minister to watch for the other anthropologies that play out in ways seen and unseen; to note the conversation in order to discover the visible and invisible realms of power being traversed; to make critical distinctions when lamentations of suffering and promises of cures declare the moral necessity of a protocol; to hold up possibilities for all of humanity that are beyond the ken of materialist or time-bound thinking; and above all to bear in mind the victory of Christ over Pilate and Caesar.

CHAPTER III

Persons in Culture and Nature

Introduction

A number of pastor-theologians wrote essays that were quite critical of the Christian church and its historical record in carrying out the anthropological consequences of its Trinitarian and Christological affirmations of faith. Looking back over the twentieth century as likeliest the bloodiest ever in human history, they were skeptical about any total reliance on Christian scripture and tradition for providing the exclusive norms of Christian ethical behavior. The wisdom of reason, experience, and even nature need to be afforded more credence in the church's advocacy of a good life for persons increasingly living in either secularized or non-Christian religious settings. Whether in its negative or positive formulation, some form of the Golden Rule's mutual reciprocity (Matthew 7:12) does enjoy virtual universal ethical favor. How can a revised anthropology serve as a more viable bridge for multicultural two-way traffic as the church seeks to work (not worship) together with all persons of good will?

Richard R. Crocker pleads for more circumspect modesty in making claims about what it means to be human. This is because such past efforts "have been plentiful, varied, and usually unsuccessful." Far more knowledge, especially in the social and natural sciences, has led to continual modifications and frequent rejections of outdated views. In Western culture, religious accounts in the Judeo-Christian tradition are no exception, especially in light of the paradigm of Darwinian evolution and space explorations. Since all forms of human knowledge are culturally conditioned, the author finds the biblical positivism of theologians like Karl Barth to be especially unhelpful in conveying Christianity to a pluralistic culture. He prefers Paul Tillich's "method of correlation" between Christianity and culture. Therefore, the liberal Protestant tradition will continue to treasure human experience as an essential element in establishing religious truth. Paradoxically, the nature of the revelation of God in Jesus Christ compels Christian believers "to honor the experience and convictions of others," as well as "to oppose anything, even Christianity itself, that violates the vulnerability of God's being, as shown in Jesus Christ."

Byron Bangert notes that Bible-based Christianity has also been an uncritical supporter of sexism, racism, and slavery. All too often, Christianity has functioned as a legitimizing ideology for an unjust social order and human oppression. Lonely prophetic voices have usually had to protest against unholy alliances between the sacred and the secular.

Theological anthropology provides an incomparable resource for this holy calling. Scripture and tradition are hardly all-sufficient resources for Christian anthropology. Today feminist theology demonstrates clearly that the exclusion of experience as a source of theological reflection is an act of ideological hegemony. Opposing church groups that are disdainful of human experience as a normative resource for theology are often guilty of using theology for their own non-theological and socially oppressive agendas.

Pamela Fickenscher likewise faults much classical anthropology for dealing "too exclusively with human beings and actors, treating the rest of God's creation as silent and inactive." An uncritically anthropocentric view of the image of God can implicitly give us license to wield our power as we wish, at the cost of ecological chaos and disasters. Our dominion over God's non-human creation needs to benefit from "moral imagination and creative responsibility" in faithful obedience to God the Creator. Here we can be guided by God's response to Adam and Eve after they have eaten from the Tree of the Knowledge of Good and Evil (Genesis 3). There are new boundaries and new duties for those moral actors who now wish to live in conformity with God's holy and loving will. Paul Santmire is approvingly cited for deploring the romantic visions of humanity in harmony with the environment but without God, in the face of the world's vulnerability in its endless cycles of life and death. Rather, saved by Christ and renewed for service, "we are free to imagine the life around us in new ways, but in ways that are always bounded by God's powerful reign."

8. *Toward a Minimalist Anthropology*

Richard R. Crocker

What we say with confidence about what it means to be human is always tentative, rarely enduring, and frequently inaccurate. Efforts to define and locate the distinctive human attributes have been plentiful, varied, and usually unsuccessful. Everyone agrees that we are like other animals, but we also seem to ourselves to be a distinctive kind of animal; thus, we have thought that we are the tool-making animal, or the language-making animal, or the symbol-making animal, or the meaning-making animal, or the praying animal.

Most of these distinctions become questionable as we learn that other animals may engage in similar behavior, although from our perspective usually in a more rudimentary form. We also find that not all human beings have these supposedly distinctive attributes; some individuals suffer a limitation of capacity, yet they are nonetheless human; other human groups and cultures may not fully exemplify the qualities by which we are defining ourselves. From a purely biological perspective, I suppose, it is possible to define human beings as those animals whose DNA conforms to a certain pattern. Recent studies have shown that human DNA is not as distinctive as we had imagined; we in fact largely share a genetic makeup with many other animals. Yet our biological genome is still capable of providing a means whereby the human species may be distinguished from other species. Unfortunately, that fact alone does not tell us what dignity attends the human animal, or which forms or conditions of human life deserve protection, or what the genetic difference from other animals signifies.

Given these limitations, we must be careful in making claims about human distinctiveness. This carefulness is prompted not only by our limitation in self-knowledge, but also by a limitation of what we know about the existential situation of other creatures. We humans seem unable to say anything about the self-awareness of other creatures. We do not know what it is, or how it is, to be a sheep or a giraffe or an amoeba. We can hypothesize that those creatures lack many aspects of what we call self-consciousness or self-awareness.[1] Indeed, as we locate the machinery of self-awareness in distinctive parts of the human brain, we can hypothesize that other animals which lack those particular neural pathways lack the capacity for self-awareness. Yet such a claim is always tentative. We really have no way of knowing about the inner life of other creatures. Bonds between human beings and certain other animals provide empathic clues of self-consciousness, but since we cannot talk to other creatures about their experience, we are limited in the ways that we can know about it.

Of course, talking to other humans is not always a simple way of finding out about their experience either. We can be deceived, misled, mistaken, or simply obtuse. Nonetheless, human beings rely upon conversation as their primary instrument for learning about the experiences of other people. When we speak different languages, it is necessary either to find a translator or to learn the other language in order to know about the experience that other people have. Thus it is understandable that language is frequently mentioned as the key distinguishing factor between humans and other animals. Whether this distinction is absolute is not proved. And it is also the case that not all human beings are able to use language. But the relative universality of language among humans, and the apparent lack of linguistic development among other creatures, makes language useful as a way of understanding human distinctiveness.

In Western culture, we have long had a way of understanding human distinctiveness by reference to the religious accounts of creation in the Jewish-Christian Bible. These mythic accounts have told human beings that they are related to other forms of life on earth by virtue of having a common creator, but that they are distinctive in being the highest form of creation — that they are in fact creatures made in the image of their creator. While the implications of this mythic account are legion, the account itself has provided a cultural template for understanding both our relatedness to other forms of life and our distinctiveness as creatures who are capable of relationship with a creator — a divine being, God. Other religions have provided other mythic templates in other cultures, but the Jewish-Christian template has been remarkably useful and stable in shaping Western assumptions about human beings for the past two millennia. This myth, this cultural template, this religious revelation (how one values it is revealed by what one chooses to call it) has been very sturdy; it has prompted human beings to develop their cultural lives with a sense of moral responsibility, sympathy for their fellow creatures most of the time, and a sense both of responsibility for the natural world and of permission to use other creatures for food, shelter, and clothing.

The major challenge to this cultural template in the West has arisen in the last 150 years from another cultural template or paradigm: Darwinian evolution. Darwin's myth provides an alternative understanding of how human beings are related to and different from other creatures. By implication, Darwin's theory assumes a process of random change that, while never providing an explanation for the origins of life or the origins of beings, does nonetheless provide an explanation for the origins of species. It is probably fair to say that Darwin's paradigm has become more widely accepted in intellectual circles today than the Christian paradigm, though there are indeed many people who seek to reconcile the two paradigms or who see them as complementary ways of understanding our existence. The wars between Darwinian evolutionists, biblical creationists, and intelligent-design theorists are fierce in some quarters and non-existent in others. Some believers in each paradigm see them as mutually exclusive ways of understanding ourselves; others see them as differing ways of understanding ourselves. A few persons might even see the paradigms as mutually reinforcing — though this is a minority view.

Without trying to sort out the relative merits and demerits of these paradigms, I am simply trying to point out that each of them is useful to many people in providing a template for understanding human nature. It is also the case that each of them is culturally embodied and limited; evolution and the Jewish/Christian creation account alike make sense only to people who have been trained in the thought patterns of Western culture. They are ways of thinking about our existence, each with implications for social organization, ethics, and religion.

One limitation of each view becomes apparent when its advocates cease to see it as a paradigm and adopt it as the truth. For these true believers, the paradigm has become the truth, and they fail to understand how anyone, given exposure to their one perspective, could reject it. This is a problem and a limitation for both perspectives, and it accounts for some of the uglier skirmishes in the culture wars of the last century. Believers in evolution may argue that they have science on their side, and science is an authority that demands obedience. Believers in the Jewish/Christian scriptures may see their story as a direct revelation from God, truer than any other account. Each side attributes an absoluteness to its understanding that makes conversation problematic. Meanwhile, each side also rightly sees that their understanding, their myth, their truth has profound implications for how society is organized, for shaping human self-perception, for defining progress and shaping hope. Because these different accounts can lead to very different practical programs of human activity, the stakes are real, and there will inevitably be arguments, competition, and conflicts as each group tries to organize the world according to the implications of its own paradigm.

Take, for example, the controversies about abortion and birth control. If one believes that human life is a form of life qualitatively no different from any other form of life, controlling human reproduction by the same rational principles one uses in other spheres of life makes sense. Terminating an unwanted pregnancy poses no moral dilemma. If, however, one believes that every human life is a gift from God, and that every human being is made in the image of God, abortion and birth control are more problematic. This is, of course, a vast over-simplification of the issues involved, but it is a basic statement of the central issue.

The central dilemma for the Christian theologian is this: now that we have come to realize that all forms of human knowledge are culturally conditioned, and that no revelation — be it scientific or religious — becomes embodied in human culture and understanding without social construction, how does it make sense to speak of revelation at all? Can one maintain that the biblical creation accounts actually embody a divine revelation about the nature of human being that is transcendent of the cultural and linguistic forms of the story? Upon what basis could one make and sustain such a claim? Is it simply a matter of the story, through a variety of historical accidents and power plays, becoming the dominant orienting myth in a large part of the world, one that has served us for better or for worse and can be defended only on pragmatic grounds? How would one make any other argument? Of course, the cultural construction of knowledge poses a similar challenge to scientific concepts that is somewhat disguised or deflected by the contemporary ascendancy of scientific power centers. I shall simply acknowledge that challenge, but my central concerns in this essay are theological.

We in this seminar have been encouraged to pay attention to Karl Barth, whose argument about human being rests entirely on his understanding that Jesus Christ is the incarnate word of God, the true human being, and therefore that human beings properly understood are those creatures to whom God speaks. While Barth's understanding is both impressive and, for many people, compelling, it suffers from what is for many a fatal flaw: it has no foundation except itself. Indeed, from Barth's point of view, it can have no foundation except itself. From a critic's point of view, it is merely self-referential assertion; why should anyone agree with his belief that Jesus is the true human being? Barth argues from within a paradigm; he never addresses the question of how one outside that paradigm is drawn into it, except to say that it happens. People find themselves addressed by God. Christians find themselves addressed by the word of God that is Jesus Christ. And as long as Barth sees himself as addressing people within that faith paradigm (as he does; his work is called *Church Dogmatics,* after all), he can be masterfully persuasive. But if one has one foot outside the paradigm, as so many of us today do, then one can never gain a grounding for the initial assumption on which the entire edifice of Barth's theology rests.

As an alternative to Barth, the Catholic tradition of natural theology argues that the elements of human reasoning, a universal aspect of human experience, can lead us to an affirmation of God's existence, although the revelation of God's nature in Jesus Christ is beyond reason. Still, this gives us, simply as human beings, a common starting place in our quest for understanding ourselves as creatures. Protestants, and particularly Calvinists, are suspicious of the adequacy of human reasoning about the nature of God; they see how easily perverted it is by the desires of those who reason. And for this observation, there is much support. But if reason cannot be our common starting point in understanding that we are creatures of God, what can be?

For me, the more compelling answer is Paul Tillich's. Tillich argued that human existence, while diverse and particular in many ways, nonetheless has certain universal dimensions, which result in human beings in all cultures asking similar questions. These questions concern the nature and purpose of existence; they are, in fact, existential questions, questions rooted in the fact of our existence. And any revelation of God comes to us as an answer to the questions we inevitably ask. While I think Tillich would agree with Barth that Jesus Christ is the supreme word of God for human beings, Tillich's way of making that claim is to show how Jesus both intensifies and answers the questions that human beings ask. There is an argument to be made on the basis of universal human experience. It is not always an easy argument or an obvious one; it will not be convincing to everyone, necessarily. But still, Tillich sees the questions that we human beings ask as a pre-requisite for the revelation of God, which has no meaning to us except as an answer to the questions that our existence forces us to ask.

Another way of expressing the difference between these two points of view (Barth's and Tillich's) is to focus on the role of experience in the development of faith. On the face of it, Barth seems to place little or no value on experience; Tillich places a great deal. For Barth, the Christian revelation does not emerge from our human experience at all; rather, it confronts, judges, defines, and shapes our experience, but from experience alone we could never get a clue. Tillich, and those in the liberal Protestant tradition, value experience more highly. Through our experience, we come to ask questions for which Christian faith provides answers. But the answers cannot compel our attention, much less our allegiance, unless they connect with the human experience from which they emerge.

Barth's most contentious claim is an anthropological one. Barth defines human beings as the creatures whom God has addressed in Jesus Christ. Jesus Christ is God's revelation of true human being. Perhaps this is true, but how would anyone know that? One can come to an appreciation of Jesus only in the same way that one comes to the appreciation of other persons: by asking questions that they answer, or by falling in love with them. From within the circle of conviction, it may well be the testimony that Jesus Christ is true human being. But that claim cannot be used as a weapon, or even as a defense, or a way of avoiding the questions that human beings ask.

Nor can the answer be assumed before the questions are fully heard. For the questions that we ask are not necessarily perverse; they are our way of being human. They are what we are created to do. And the answers that become compelling to us are never compelled; rather, they emerge as truthful, ready to be proclaimed as part of the universal human conversation. Their truth is not denied in conversation, but enhanced as others probe our convictions, test them, and challenge them. And in the course of that human conversation, the convictions that we hold are slowly modified, so that our part of the conversation can become less defensive, more open, and more loving.

That, at least, is what liberal Protestants continue to believe, humbly, but with open tenacity. Some critics see in this liberal stance (as Barth apparently did) a lack of awareness of sin. But liberal Protestants do not have to be unaware that sin corrupts all our intentions and capacities to be open and loving, and to see things from any position other than our own. But the fact of sin does not make dialogue hopeless. In fact, liberals believe that the fact of sin makes dialogue all the more necessary, precisely because our selfishness otherwise would totally dominate our actions. And the chief challenge to that open liberal tenacity is the kind of sin expressed by any other partners in conversation who are so convinced of the truth of their own position that they will not listen to the experience of others.

But of course many have seen the very openness of liberal Protestant Christianity as leading to its demise. Neo-orthodox and evangelical theologians have scorned its identification with secular cultures, seeing it at best as an identification with the spirit of the age and at worst as a demonic threat to genuine Christianity. On a popular level, its influence seems to have waned. Mainline Protestant churches have declined in number while more evangelical and conservative churches have grown. This observation ignores the fact, however, that the proportion of non-affiliated persons has grown fastest of all. In an era when religious unbelief or indifference seems powerful, it is tempting for believers to circle the wagons. This stance is, of course, not an expression of liberal Christianity, which has always felt its mission to consist as much in engaging the world as in resisting it.

The dilemma is theological, cultural, and anthropological. If human beings are creatures, or simply beings, who ask questions, then how is one to evaluate their answers to what we can call existential and theological questions? Adherents of many religious traditions, including parts of Christianity, believe that answers have been revealed to them that essentially defy evaluation by any universally accessible standard. Other, entirely secular perspectives have given up on ultimate answers altogether, assuming that the tentative answers of the secular mind take them as far as the human mind is capable of going.

In these conflicts, liberal Christianity takes yet a third position. It holds fast to the revelation of God in Jesus Christ, saying that Jesus shows us who God is; further, it believes that, given enough dialogue in the proper spirit, the claim that Jesus is the revelation of God can become meaningful and convincing to all persons. And yet, paradoxically, the nature of the revelation of God in Jesus compels Christian believers to honor the experience and convictions of others, and to oppose anything, even Christianity itself, that violates the vulnerability of God's being as shown in Jesus Christ. This is a subtle point upon which to build an institution; it is no wonder that so few have been able to sustain it. In fact, it is a wonder that any institutions embodying this faith exist at all, since it is the nature of institutions to establish themselves, protect themselves, and perpetuate themselves at almost any cost.

9. Theological Anthropology in a New Day

Byron C. Bangert

Introduction

In an essay published in *The Christian Century* more than thirty years ago, Sheila Collins observed,

> Throughout history — so textual critics and anthropologists agree — societies have elevated certain of their social infrastructures to the realm of belief; and such belief systems in turn have become the justification for the continuation of the social structures from which they sprang. As sophisticated Christians, I think we all realize that Christianity, though revelatory, has not been without its cultural taint.[2]

Collins's immediate purpose in her essay is to make a case for feminist theology, based on evidences of patriarchy and its attendant subordination of women to men within the Christian scriptures and tradition. Her claim regarding the relationship between social infrastructures and systems of belief, however, is much more widely applicable. For example, those who study economics with a critical eye risk the discovery that free-market economic theory provides a far from accurate description of economic events "on the ground." The components of the theory may be — perhaps necessarily are — sufficiently correlated to actual economic entities and systems to appear to provide a realistic model of actual economic activity. Nonetheless, the theory functions much more effectively as an ideological justification for maintaining key features of the capitalist economy than as a complete or accurate account of what is going on.

Those who have studied the relationship between race and religion in America likewise know that biblical interpreters in slaveholding states tended to find in their scriptures sufficient theological justification for the practice of slavery, while biblical interpreters in non-slaveholding states more often concluded from the same scriptures that slavery violated the laws of God. A similar pattern and dynamic is being repeated today in many church denominations as they struggle over the question of the appropriate status of gay and lesbian persons in church life and society. Traditional interpreters claim scriptural and theological warrant for proscribing homosexual relations, and thus legitimate the exclusion on non-celibate gay and lesbian persons from church office and, in some cases, even membership. Interpreters sympathetic to the claims and circumstances of the gay and lesbian persons in their midst find themselves offering new justifications based on revised exegetical and theological understanding of the accepted meaning and authority of the ancient texts.

Theories and systems of belief function not only as reflections or models of actual practices, systems, and structures, but also as justifications for those practices, systems, and structures. Collins minces no words when she applies this insight to gender relations:

> Just as the theory of the divine right of kings served to legitimize a feudal system which kept a vast majority of the people in subjection and poverty, so the system of male-oriented symbols, doctrines and taboos in the Judeo-Christian tradition has served to keep females in subjection to men and in spiritual, if not always physical, poverty.[3]

I agree with Collins on this point, and I share most of the concerns of feminist theologians. However, the point of my essay is not to advance a specifically feminist agenda. My intention is to explore the question of theological anthropology in light of the critical insight that informs Collins's work. More specifically, the claim here is that Christian theology, though revelatory, must also be critically examined as a belief system or ideology that shares the traits of other belief systems and ideologies. The historical and cultural contexts in which Christian theology has emerged and developed have left their distinctive marks upon it. Christian theology has consequently served in many and various ways to legitimate and justify the patterns, practices, and power distributions of the social orders of its originating and developing contexts.

There are other ways to state the first part of this claim. For example, one may say that Christian theology is historically contingent and culturally conditioned. When stated in this way, the focus of concern tends to be directed toward the status of the truth claims that Christian theology makes. The central question becomes, "How does one differentiate between the 'wheat' of true revelation and the 'chaff' of cultural taint in the claims of Christianity?" I am certainly interested in this question, but I want to insist that it is not an academic question. Nor is it only a strictly theological question. That is to say, it is not only a question regarding what we as Christians are to believe. It is a question that has implications for how we as Christians are to live.

Why Theology Matters

This brings us to the second part of the above claim, namely, that Christian theology also functions to a considerable extent as a legitimizing ideology for the social order. It is most important to recognize that this claim is not tantamount to an indictment of Christian theology. There is much in our prevailing social order that we presumably desire to legitimate and that we might defend on Christian grounds. There are many values and practices in our social existence for which it is useful to invoke the justifications of Christian theology. The claim regarding the role of theology in justifying existing social arrangements does become something of an indictment, however, whenever it becomes clear that there is something undesirable about the social order that nevertheless receives continuing legitimation from Christian theological doctrine, symbol, or tradition.

In other words, Christian theology has profound ethical significance. In his well-known essay "Human Being," theologian David H. Kelsey provides a brief account of the development of doctrine of theological anthropology within Christianity. In a passage on the social dimension of human nature, he notes the contributions of Augustine and Aquinas to what he calls the "classic formulation" of the doctrine. Noting ways in which Augustine argued for the hierarchical subordination of women to men, and the further claims of Aquinas that women are deficient expressions of human nature, Kelsey calmly yet pointedly observes,

> At this point both moral and theological considerations raise radical doubts about the adequacy of the classic formulation of the doctrine of human nature. One has to ask whether it is moral to hold a view that has caused so much human anguish.[4]

Kelsey assumes, without further argument, that Christian theological beliefs have ethical implications. I might have begun this essay with this assumption, an assumption that I cannot imagine will meet with disagreement from anyone who believes that theology matters. But because I am going to reflect at some length upon the practical, moral, and ethical implications of Christian beliefs, it seemed useful to provide some indication of how it is that beliefs matter. In Sheila Collins's terms, beliefs matter because they provide legitimation and justification for certain — and by implication, fail to do so for other — practices, systems, and structures within the social order. If Collins is wrong, then it is not clear that theology is of any consequence at all.

It may appear that I am denying to theology any role as social critique. To the contrary, I will contend that this is a crucial role for theology today. But I do not imagine theology playing this role except as a dissenting voice, emerging from a particular place and time, within the larger society. It is possible for theology to play this role precisely because no society is uniformly ordered, no legitimating belief system is equally compelling upon all members of a society. (Primitive societies might constitute an exception, but no one from such a society will be reading this essay!) Within any society or social order one can expect to find those whose beliefs are rooted in a different constellation of life experiences from that of the prevailing majority or dominating minority. The stories of Israel and of Christianity are replete with instances of lonely prophetic voices, drawing upon shared religious traditions, yet dissenting from contemporary religious practices, doctrines, and legitimations. Jesus of Nazareth stands clearly within this "dissenting tradition" of what later generations have come to regard as faithful witness. The Protestant reformers doubtless saw themselves as Christians who were laying claim to this "dissenting tradition" as well. Their theological reformulations of the dominant traditions were not thereby exempt from historical contingency and cultural condition. Nonetheless, they were clearly engaged in theological and social critique of a sort that made a real difference.

The point to be underscored here is that theology, as a system of beliefs, ideas, and symbols, is a matter of ethical significance precisely because it matters. It matters in that it makes a difference in terms of how we perceive, understand, and act upon the question of how we are to live. Theology matters in that it provides, or fails to provide, legitimation and justification for social patterns, structures, and practices. Alternatively, at times theology matters precisely because it is able to provide a critique that contributes to the transformation of prevailing social arrangements and ways of being.

The Critical Role of Theological Anthropology

Now, Christian theology has many facets. It has traditionally been constituted of many doctrines. These doctrines do not stand alone, but contribute to a comprehensive theological system or worldview. Thus it is difficult, if not impossible, to extract and assess any single doctrine in isolation from other doctrines. This is especially true of theological anthropology, or the Christian doctrine of humankind. There are at least two primary ways to elaborate a doctrine of humankind. The classic approach, as Kelsey notes, has been to draw upon Genesis 1–3, which includes the declaration that human beings have been created in the image of God. There is no consensus among biblical scholars or theologians regarding the meaning of the *imago Dei.* Thus, one of the tasks of theological anthropology is to provide an interpretation of the *imago Dei* idea. It is highly likely, therefore, that whatever conclusions one reaches pertaining to theological anthropology will have immediate implications for one's understanding of God, in whose image humankind has been created. And vice versa.

Theological anthropology may also be elaborated in terms of the person of Jesus, who is identified by the tradition as both the Son of God and "true" human. More contemporary theology often speaks of Jesus as "fully human." Thus, in Jesus, Christians claim to see the human being as God intended each of us to be. Because Jesus is also identified as Son of God, and even "true" God, the link here between human self-perception and self-understanding and our understanding of God's character and being could hardly be more intimate or immediate. Whether elaborated in terms of the "image of God" or in terms of the "fully human" Jesus, our theological anthropology, or doctrine of humankind, is bound to have direct and possibly profound significance for our doctrine of God.[5]

It is hardly possible to anticipate and address every objection that may be raised to the approach taken here. Doubtless there are those who would object to this and any other kind of "theology from below." They would insist that the Christian doctrine of God must not be contingent upon or derivative of a Christian doctrine of humankind in any way. The doctrine of God, in their view, must be epistemologically privileged over any other doctrine. But consider the implications of such theological immunity in view of the interrelatedness of all theological doctrines. Such a stance would seem to be tantamount to a refusal to articulate or elaborate any theological doctrine apart from what has already come to be accepted as revealed in scripture and tradition. I have heard it argued with respect to the subordination of women, for example, that if scripture is marked by patriarchy and female subordination, God must have wanted it that way. Moreover, God may appropriately be viewed as the supreme patriarch, just as "He" always has been in both scripture and tradition. The argument of this essay will leave little favorable impression upon those who see matters so. It is my view that scripture and tradition are hardly all-sufficient sources for Christian theology. In fact, neither those whose witness has become scripture nor the formulators of tradition were ever themselves so constrained by received tradition.

Let me be clear that this essay does not attempt to develop a full-fledged theological anthropology. I have a more limited, a more critical objective — to argue for the reformulation of Christian theology in light of the moral and ethical failures of theological anthropology. Socrates maintained that we should follow the argument where it leads, and I agree, but the argument I am making leads where few Christians seem prepared to go. We have come to a fork in the road. One way follows the argument toward a major reformulation of Christian theology. The other way dead-ends, or simply circles back upon itself. We are faced with a decision of profoundly moral and ethical significance. We must ask ourselves whether it is acceptable to hold to any theological view irrespective of its implications for the ordering of human life.[6]

As previously noted, David Kelsey concludes from his discussion of the classic formulations of theological anthropology by Augustine and Aquinas, "One has to ask whether it is moral to hold a [theological] view that has caused so much human anguish." In the view taken here, it is not. Nor does it seem moral to hold to any other theological view whose effect upon human existence is apparently negative, in part or as a whole. A negative effect may be one that distorts, diminishes, trivializes, inflates, frustrates, abuses, impairs, estranges, isolates, or polarizes human beings in their self-understanding and relationship with one another. Theology matters, and good theology contributes to a proper social ordering and an appropriate human flourishing.

This is not to say that the *only* proper concern of Christian theology is human existence. It is to say that human existence is *always and inescapably* a proper concern of Christian theology. We cannot responsibly "do" theology without regard for its implications for human existence. Of course, we cannot responsibly "do" theology without regard for the rest of existence, either. Theological anthropology need not be, and in my view should never be, anthropocentric. But insofar as theological anthropology is about human beings, it must be concerned about their good. Christians have every reason to believe that God desires their good, and the good of all others — indeed, the good of all Creation. The questions that theological anthropology must address have to do with what it is to be human, and what it is that constitutes the human good. There is much that scripture and tradition have to say by way of answers to these questions. However, the particular significance of theological anthropology for Christian theology as a whole derives from the fact that any adequate formulation of the human condition and the human good requires us to take into consideration the full range of human experience and human knowledge as data for theology.

Appropriating the Feminist Critique

Nowhere have the shortcomings — indeed, the moral failures — of classical theological anthropology and Christian theology in general been more clearly and compellingly exposed than in the work of the feminist theologians. Feminist theologians have contributed many insights to contemporary theological work, but perhaps above all they have contributed their experience. That is to say, they have contributed their experience as female rather than male, as subordinate rather than dominant, as often abused or oppressed rather than abusive or in control, as preoccupied with trivialities rather than engaged in master projects, and so on. Feminists, including feminist theologians, have contributed enormously to our understanding of what it means to be human, as well as what it means to be de-humanized. Methodologically, they have convincingly argued for the necessity of human experience — their own human experience, but also the experience of all human beings — as an indispensable datum of theology. Moreover, they have made the case that the exclusion of experience as a source of theological reflection is an act of hegemony. As theologian Mary Pellauer has put it, "As a feminist theologian, I claim that the extent to which any theology obscures its experiential base is the extent to which it participates in patriarchy."[7]

There are reasons, in other words, why experience is often excluded as a source of theological reflection and knowledge, and those reasons have to do with the maintenance and legitimation of an existing social order. The notably distinguishing feature of that social order, for Pellauer, is patriarchy. In my own experience, theology also functions to maintain other forms of social and political hegemony. Most often this is done in subtle, perhaps even unwitting, ways. Those in charge of the organs of decision-making and communication of virtually any religious organization can be counted on to employ theology in ways that tap into shared traditions and understandings. We may even expect this of them and commend them for it. When they do so, however, those in charge are also providing for their own justification and legitimation as holders of power. That is to say, those who hold power typically also possess the ideological means to legitimate their power. For that reason, power relationships usually need to be changed in order to effect social and theological change, as feminist theologians have clearly recognized (thus the need for women clergy).

Sometimes theology is used in what seem to be deliberately invidious ways. The Presbyterian Lay Committee is one of a number of politically and socially right-wing organizations that uses theology, including the traditional creeds and its own version of orthodoxy, to attack, ridicule, marginalize, and exclude those whose theological or social perspectives call for a way of being Christian that is inclusive with respect to sexual orientation, fully respectful of other faith traditions, politically liberal, theologically innovative, or critical of capitalism and nationalism as well as patriarchy. Such use of theology is profoundly immoral, whether or not it bears epistemological scrutiny on its own terms — that is, whether or not it is a faithful articulation of what it regards to be its inherited and historically legitimated tradition. It should be no surprise that the Presbyterian Lay Committee leadership is utterly disdainful of human experience as a normative resource for theology.

10. Moral Imagination and Creative Responsibility

Pamela Fickenscher

In popular literature today, creativity is celebrated as an essentially human trait, one to be nurtured, or "discovered" by accountants and artists alike. Business books trumpet that creativity is the driving force behind all market success. Many Americans believe they "have a book in them," and bookshelves are bursting with exercises and instructions for taping into one's creative powers. Nevertheless, our imagination as a society seems relatively stunted when it comes to matters of deepest significance. Economic possibilities beyond a consumer capitalist system have all but disappeared from serious discussion. We hear constant reports about the spread of AIDS in Africa, ethnic rivalries that go on for generations, and continued environmental degradation. Where are the imaginative approaches to these problems? How might we live in harmony with one another and with the rest of Creation? How might we build cities that honor both the economic needs of people and the ecological complexity of the world around us? How might marriages and families be strengthened in an age of individualism? How might a society that does not discriminate on the basis of creed still hold to common assumptions about what constitutes the good life? Why do so many imagine they can write a novel, yet so few imagine a new solution to these pressing questions?

Part of the problem may be in the triumph of technique and technology of our century. While hundreds of "how to" books exist on everything from becoming a writer to finding a spouse, fine literature itself is read less frequently. Social scientists Leon and Amy Kass, in a study of courtship in the modern era, argue that it is a failure of imagination that most deeply affects young people as they begin to build intimate relationships.[8] While popular self-help and school curricula focus on practical "how-to's," the Kasses contend that the dearth of fictional and factual examples of loving, committed relationships leaves young people uncertain of what they might hope for in love. In the name of "realism," what little education is offered about marriage focuses on statistics of divorce, probabilities for success, sexual education, family planning skills, and perhaps techniques for communication. The topic of what intimacy is for, the richness of long-term companionship, and the possibility of service to the larger world are rarely addressed. Literature that once was taught to convey values and encourage dreams of love is now divorced from its subject in most schools.

I intend to argue that the role of moral imagination is essential in developing right relationships with the rest of Creation and with God. Christian theology has a unique contribution to make in the discussion about moral imagination because we understand ourselves as both responsible co-creators and sinful creatures. Secular modern thinking tends to treat humankind alone as subjects, while Creation is merely backdrop, scenery for the human drama. This realism treats any language about the complexity of Creation as romantic or poetic. Christian thought maintains that the Creator, not humankind, is the prime subject, but much classical theology has dealt exclusively with human beings as creatures and actors, treating the rest of God's Creation as silent and inactive. The idea that relationships of reciprocity might occur between God and other creatures is seldom treated with seriousness. Postmodern thinking and movements such as "deep ecology" have questioned the anthropocentrism of these perspectives, but usually without any realistic consideration of humanity's unique position in relationship to God and the world.

Taking the rest of Creation seriously in our theology forces us immediately into questions of anthropology. We, too, are creatures, yet we also wield enormous creative power over our world. We share a common home with all that God has made, and yet the Scriptures maintain that we have a unique relationship to God, a representative role as the *imago Dei,* those given dominion over the rest of Creation. This role does not strip the rest of Creation of its agency, nor does it give us license to wield our power as we wish. Our powers are frequently more destructive than creative; indeed, it is far easier for a human being to take life than to give it. One can much more easily tear down than build up. In this regard we appear to be limited, not entirely like God. Moreover, the rest of Creation holds its own power over us, often overcoming our best efforts to predict, contain, and minimize its effects on us. We have only begun to understand the complexity of the global climate, ecosystems, and the oceans. The ability to control them is far beyond our reach.

Truly encountering nature's complexity — and its threat — makes us face our own limits and acknowledge God's greater power. This ability to acknowledge that we are not omnipotent becomes increasingly difficult in our scientific age, when more and more of life's mysteries are reduced to chemical and physical formulas. While some insist that scientific knowledge merely increases our wonder at nature's complexity and reveals one deeper mystery after another, others worry that our desire to master nature will outstrip any caution about meddling in matters of life and death. Some romantic reactions to the destructiveness of human greed and the sterility of technology have resulted in philosophies that want to minimize humanity's power over Creation and limit the uniqueness of humanity's role. "We shouldn't play God" is a frequent chorus among those who fear scientific mastery over the human genome. But "playing" God is, in fact, what many of our creative activities rightly do. We cannot design 44,000 beetles, as the Creator did, but we continually design, create, compose, and improvise from the palette of colors, sounds, words, and materials available to us. The difference in our creative powers is increasingly not in technique or material, but in our ability to recognize limits and responsibility for the results.

In a world where creativity is sometimes secular shorthand for a theology of human potential, Christians must understand imagination in light of our proper place in Creation. We are made in God's image, endowed with creative abilities and freedom to use them for evil or good. Yet we are also charged with "dominion" over the earth, given responsibility for the care of the garden in which we are placed. Our imagination must therefore be shaped by our moral responsibility to the Creator for all of Creation — not only our fellow human beings, but also the complex planet on which we live. This moral imagination is shaped and given its bounds by the biblical story, which reminds us of our limits as well as our glory, and which calls us to acknowledge God's power above our own at every turn.

Play God: Frankenstein and Creative Responsibility

Mary Shelley's *Frankenstein,* written in the nineteenth century, was a prescient fable about the tendency of human scientific knowledge to outstrip our moral ability to deal with what we have created. Although frequently cited as a warning against "playing God," Shelley's tale does not, in fact, condemn the use of sophisticated science. According to many standards, in fact, Frankenstein's monster is a success. It is clear that he is capable of communication, sensitivity, and appreciation of beauty, and is filled with a longing for human relationship. However, because his creator abandons him almost immediately after he comes to life, the monster behaves in increasingly vindictive and violent ways, constantly threatening Frankenstein's own happiness and security.

Victor Frankenstein, ironically named, is a picture of creative failure and abandoned responsibility. His fate is foreshadowed even as he begins his research into the secrets of life. He describes his studies as obsessive, cutting him off from friends and family at home and finally making it impossible for him to enjoy even the beauties of nature. His creation takes place in a sort of vacuum, with no accountability to others; his own delight in newfound power and fantasies of God-like status preoccupy all his thoughts. He imagines his world after his creative triumph in utopian ways, but is unable to apply that imagination to empathize with those around him. "A new species would bless me as its Creator and source; many happy and excellent natures would owe their being to me. No father could claim the gratitude of his child so completely as I should deserve theirs."[9] This fantasy lives only as long as his creature is not alive; as soon as the monster lives, Victor suffers a nervous breakdown.

Popular culture has tended to leave out the crucial portion of the novel, in which the monster, after years of wandering, finally has a conversation with Victor Frankenstein. He describes his growing consciousness of other human beings, the acquisition of language, great hope for human interaction, and finally despair and rage as he is denied the companionship of others. He develops an appreciation for music and literature, and describes his encounter with *Paradise Lost:*

> Like Adam, I was apparently united by no link to any other being in existence; but his state was far different from mine in every other respect. He had come forth from the hands of God a perfect creature, happy

> and prosperous, guarded by the special care of his Creator; he was allowed to converse with and acquire knowledge from beings of a superior nature, but I was wretched, helpless, and alone.[10]

Unlike human beings, Frankenstein's monster is given no name by his creator, no instruction in how to live, and finally no companion like himself. It is this longing for a companion — and his demand that his maker give him one — that finally drives him to seek revenge against Frankenstein. In the end, the monster deliberately deprives Victor of the people he loves the most.

Victor's story is not simply a tale of scientific failure. It is framed in the novel by the correspondence of another ambitious young man, Walton, who is lonely but willing to sacrifice relationships for the sake of pursuing personal glory. Walton's own change of heart at novel's end suggests that Victor's greatest failing is not merely pride, but lack of relationship. Victor fails to deal with the consequences of his creation's shortcomings; he fails — though given ample opportunity — to develop a relationship with the creature and thus minimize his rage; he fails to tell his closest friends of his failure and thus endangers their lives. Once events set course in an unexpected direction, Frankenstein is repeatedly unable to imagine an outcome in which he could take responsibility for what he has done.

Harold Bloom argues that in matters of moral and relational sensitivity, the monster, in fact, excels his creator. He is more sensitive to art and music, more in touch with his emotions and need for companionship. He, in fact, is the "total form of Frankenstein's creative power and is *more imaginative* than his creator. . . . Frankenstein is the mind and emotions turned in on themselves, and his creature is the mind and emotions turned imaginatively outward, seeking a greater humanization toward confrontation with other selves."[11] The isolation of the monster, Bloom argues, is a common theme in romantic literature, but Frankenstein's monster is deprived of the one great release afforded most tragic romantic figures: he cannot return to a "natural" state, most frequently signified by the ocean. Since he has had no natural birth, his story ends instead in the frozen Arctic, on a pyre of his own making.[12]

If God is the model of creative responsibility and relationship with what one has made, then Genesis 3 offers an alternate scenario to how we respond when our creative works go awry. After Adam and Eve have eaten of the Tree of the Knowledge of Good and Evil, God's response is deliberate:

1. God seeks the creature out. The first question asked is not "What have you done?" but "Where are you?" The shame that Adam and Eve immediately feel causes them to hide, and the Creator takes the initiative in finding them.
2. God recognizes their failure and names it: "Have you eaten of the tree?" Whereas the humans hide from their actions and avoid admission, God speaks immediately of what has occurred.
3. God refuses to engage in their attempts to excuse themselves by blaming someone else.
4. God describes the consequences of their actions. Moving back up the "chain of blame" Adam and Eve create — snake, woman, man — God speaks of their future in unadorned truth.
5. God provides care in the new situation of vulnerability. Although shame at their nakedness is the first sign that they have exceeded boundaries set for them, God makes allowances for this state and clothes them.
6. God sets new boundaries to prevent further harm. Adam and Eve are cast from the garden, and cherubim guard the tree of life.

By contrast, Victor's response to the monster is — not surprisingly — much more like that of Adam and Eve after eating from the tree. He is ashamed and fearful of what he has done. He tells no one and spends the rest of his days hiding from the consequences. Because he runs from what he has done, he cannot in any way contain the damage done by the monster. His life ceases to contain joy and love and instead is fixated on avoiding his failure. He loses his ability to appreciate beauty. Having trespassed in the knowledge of creating life, he is ill equipped to take on that responsibility, and yet unable to return to his previous innocent state.

As readers, we follow his story constantly wondering, "What if he did provide the monster with a companion?" or "What if, instead of accepting enmity, he attempted to reconcile with the creature and build a relationship?" At many points in the tale we can imagine such a result, but in a supreme use of dramatic irony, Shelley never allows Victor to undergo such a change of heart. Only Walton, the narrator who relates the tale to us, begins to question his personal ambition and imagine turning back from a course (quite literally, as a ship's captain) that would endanger both himself and his crew.

Pride, or "playing God," is the sin which many ethicists fear most when considering scientific advances of this century. We are admonished to beware of using the technical knowledge that we have, for fear of unseen consequences. A potent example is in animal (including, ultimately, human) cloning, which currently requires multiple failures before a single viable creature survives. Is the victory of this single creation worth the failure that precedes it? When such techniques are applied to human beings, are we prepared to deal with the myriad of things that might go wrong? Our imaginations can — and in pop culture have — run amok with visions of monstrous creations and horribly tragic outcomes.[13] Some argue that such negativity overlooks the possible benefits of such technologies. But unless we are able to deal honestly and imaginatively with the possibilities for both failure and success, we fail to take our creative powers seriously.

The importance of human imagination and creativity can be kept in perspective only by its comparison with divine creative power. Human beings can indeed imagine, design, fashion, mold and change their environment and even the creatures around them in astonishing ways; however, this power is not creation *ex nihilo,* nor is it able to overcome the ultimate limit placed upon all human life: death. Utopian visions fail most obviously when we face our fear of death — both our own mortality and the prevalence of death throughout the natural world.

Against Romantic Simplicity

Paul Santmire argues in *Nature Reborn* that romantic visions of man in harmony with his environment are particularly problematic when we attempt to envision a path forward from the current state of affairs.[14] Environmental texts are full of idealized images of agrarian communities, Native American respect for life, and poetic appreciation of nature's complexity. Few thinkers, however, have attempted to bridge the gap between the concrete difficulties of "cleanup" and the ideal relationships we envision. On a theological level, many thinkers would rather do away with the very notion of human dominion rather than acknowledge its practical truth in a world where human ability to alter the environment exceeds that of any other species. Why is it so difficult to take the non-human world at face value, acknowledging both its strangeness and its vulnerability?

Santmire takes American transcendentalists as a prime example of the failure of romantic visions to adequately deal with nature. Henry David Thoreau believed he fully appreciated the natural world as long as he remained in his relatively domestic retreat at Walden. That changed when he traveled to Maine. There, hiking in real wilderness, he encountered black flies, and lost some of his love of "the wild."[15] But black flies, Santmire points out, are precisely the point of experiencing wilderness. "Nature, if we see it with eyes wide open, is the world of death par excellence."[16] Suffering and death are part of the natural order, if suffering is defined as the hardship of finding food and the danger of being food for another creature. Our very denial of death, our instinctive response that we don't deserve such treatment, cuts us off from real appreciation of the complexity of the Creation.

Does this mean that in order to move beyond death denial, we must submit to insect bites, sharing our homes with rodents, or place ourselves at the mercy of the elements without the aid of technology? Of course not. Deep ecology, which places human beings on the same level as the rest of Creation, cannot even reconcile itself with a Garden of Eden anthropology of *imago Dei,* much less with the post-fall enmity between the snake and the woman. But perhaps in order to have proper "dominion" over the rest of Creation, we need a deeper appreciation of how, without God, death rules our world, for only then do we see that now death has no more dominion over us who are saved in Christ. It is our role as stewards of the earth, God's representatives to Creation, to care for that world. Since God, not death, reigns over us, we are free to imagine life around us in new ways, but ways that are always bounded by God's powerful reign.

PART TWO

FAITHFUL AND PRUDENT MANAGERS

CHAPTER IV

Embodied Persons

Introduction

Most of the pastor-theologians identified strongly with their colleagues' complaint that funerals often expose the raw nerve of perennial heresy that co-exists with the authentic piety of the grieving relatives and friends of the deceased within the church. All too many Christians, especially in the presence of the death of a loved one, unwittingly cling to the Platonic view of an immortal soul released from a mortal body, their dualistic anthropology totally inconsistent with their other orthodox, Trinitarian views of creation, redemption and sanctification. The Gnostic body-soul dualism has been falsely correlated with the Pauline opposition of "flesh and Spirit," sin and righteousness (Romans 7–8), confusing and compromising both. At stake in Christian anthropology is our confession of "the resurrection of the body" in the Apostles' Creed.

Of course, sermons at gravesides are no occasion for providing erudite elucidations of *sarx, sōma,* and *pneuma.* Nevertheless, there are many less distraught times in the ongoing teaching ministry of pastor-theologians to proclaim the whole counsel of God on the finality of the death of the old "earthly, physical" body and the resurrection hope of a new "heavenly, spiritual" body of the Christian "soul" (self). Paul's gospel clearly promises that death will be swallowed up in a future victory: "For the perishable body must put on imperishability, and the mortal body must put on immortality" (1 Corinthians 15:35-58).

Scott Hoezee contends that "even in the light of contemporary science, belief in a real human soul is wholly warranted. Further, in the end I wish to assert that this soul can indeed be preserved by God after the death of the body in a way that ensures both conscious existence in the intermediate state and a complete resurrection of the whole person when God's Kingdom fully comes in Christ Jesus."

The essay excerpt concentrates on the author's view of the nature of a soul from a strictly biblical point of view. The Genesis account clarifies that God formed the body first, complete with a brain, and the person emerged only after that body was brought to life by the breath of God. Hence there is no biblical warrant for the Greek idea of a pre-existing immortal soul. Rather, it is here proposed that the soul (or essence) of the person emerges as a result of the biological components coming together in distinctly human ways. Many features of human life resist reduction to mere biology. There is within the human person a "high-order pattern of information" which may well be where the essence of that person resides over and above the physical matter that this information patterns. This "soul" has substantial, ontological reality. After someone dies, the soul or "living pattern" of the person is what God can and will preserve until that time when it will once more have a new body to form and pattern in the resurrection of the dead.

The very first sentence of David Miles's completed essay centers on "the last words spoken by a man about to die." (Ironically, a few days later, Miles himself entered the Church Triumphant along with his father after their involvement in a fatal automobile accident.) These words uttered by a thief hanging on the cross beside the crucified Jesus express the frequent human prayer in the biblical witness to be "remembered" by God. Beyond simplistic anthropomorphism is the confessed miracle that the eternal God graciously chooses to participate "in time" with humanity, both with Israel and in the incarnate Christ. Time and eternity intersect in the mighty acts of God. Regarding the unique nature of God's "memory," Bernard Lonergan suggests that God is *simul* (at once) with all created beings that are, were, and will be, in the created universe. Jesus declares that the Creator Lord is "God not of the dead, but of the living; for to him all therein are alive" (Luke 20:38). While there are obvious dangers in speaking indiscriminately of eternal life as "being held in God's memory," the author favors the distinctively Trinitarian theology of Robert Jenson. There one can affirm the otherness of the Son from the Father, and thereby also the gift of our baptismal incorporation into that divine relationship which can be graciously "remembered."

J. Harold McKeithen, Jr. explores the soul's nature in repudiation of two erroneous views: materialism and dualism. Instead, he uses the terms *mind, soul,* and *self* interchangeably. First he rejects the scientific materialism of Edward O. Wilson. Here, "natural selection and neurobiological processes combine to produce and govern all aspects of human being." Religious belief is genetically determined and will diminish with the maturation of the social sciences into predictive disciplines. The research of John Hick and Paul Badham reject the reduction of human beings to physical properties and processes. Indeed, scientism is deemed a "self-refuting theory" in principle, and guilty of the unscientific disregard of mystical and parapsychological phenomena in practice. Non-reductive physicalism (Nancey Murphy and Warren Brown) affirms the human's distinguishing capacities and functions that give rise to morality and spirituality. In opposing dualism, the physical and the non-physical are interdependent aspects of a complex human person. The "soul" may therefore be viewed as "the personal capacity for and experience of one's relatedness to the self, to others, and to God."

11. *The Soul and Science*

Scott Hoezee

But Is It a Soul?

There are strong reasons, based on the science of cosmic and human origins, to embrace as likely the probability that what explains the existence of life, especially of human life in this world, is the intentional crafting of the universe by a God whose goal all along was to end up with conscious creatures capable of thought and communication, including communication with God. There clearly is a non-biological dimension to human rationality. We'd be nothing without our physical brains, but *with* such a complex of biological and neurological wonders inside our heads we find it possible to convey and receive information which resists reduction to the merely biological. Who we are, what our personalities are like, and the ways by which outside information from other people and, Christians believe, from God create and shape entities that are physical at their base but metaphysical in their operations and results.

But is this extra dimension to humanity a "soul" in any traditional, theological sense of that word — or at least does all of this hint at or point to some kind of non-physical entity that each person possesses beyond sheer biology? If "soul" is defined as some non-physical, extra something God at some point pours into a human body, then the answer would be "No." Although I would assert that the necessary biological components of any given human person give rise to something that in the end goes beyond the physical, it should be obvious that, even so, the biological components need to be there *first* as that out of which our non-biological essence emerges. Hence, no biological hardware, no soul — at least in the sense that no soul would arise without the prior existence of a human body complete with that marvelously complex unit called the brain. In a sense, this is a chicken-and-the-egg scenario: could God create a chicken without ever having the chick first grow in an egg? Presumably God could do so, but God typically does not do it this way. The normal route is for the egg to come first and that egg then becomes the necessary prior condition required for the emergence of a chicken. So also here: could God create a human soul without its ever having been a body? Presumably God could do that, but there is no evidence that God does so. Even the more picturesque account of Genesis makes it clear that God formed the body first and the person emerged only after that body was brought to life by the breath of God. The soul of Adam did not float and flit around in God's head waiting for the Almighty to create a body into which this disembodied essence could then be poured. (I am aware, however, that very intelligent dualist anthropologies have posited that the *nephesh* or *ruach* which God breathed into Adam's nostrils is a kind of third "something" after all — a soul which did indeed get added to the physical matter. At the very least I see the tight connection between the physical body, which came first, and the subsequent quickening of that matter as evidence that even biblically you do not find "souls" which exist prior to conception and the emergence of the physical being.)

But this much ought not to be too controversial or surprising from a strictly biblical point of view; there is no biblical warrant for the Greek idea of a pre-existing immortal soul. Although a large swath of the Christian theological tradition has envisioned the ongoing existence of the soul before the human person is conceived, this idea has not won orthodox status. At the very least it seems that the main lines of the tradition have associated the creation (or the imputation) of a human soul with the physical creation of the human body. My model proposes a similar association of body with soul, but with the soul (or essence) of the person emerging as a *result* of the biological components coming together and functioning in distinctly human ways, rather than something which gets added on irrespective of the physical processes of human existence, and particularly of the human brain.

But let us delve a bit more deeply into precisely what "emerges" out of the biological of human existence — out of those conditions which I have called necessary but not sufficient to explain the whole of human nature. A good place to begin this inquiry is with a couple of quick facts about the human brain as we know it. As most people now know, scientists consider the human brain to be the single most complex organism ever discovered. The number of individual neurons within a single human brain is well into the trillions. Staggering though that fact is, what becomes even more amazing is the way those neurons can and must work together. Although there is some disagreement in the scientific community over precisely how to add up these figures, it is the interconnections (and the possibilities for varying scenarios of neural interconnections) that bring the true wonder of the human brain to the forefront.

It is estimated that the total number of atoms in the known universe is something like 10^{18} atoms (a "pretty big number," as John Polkinghorne once commented in a rather grand understatement). Yet the total number of possible ways for connecting and inter-connecting those trillions of neurons in a *single* human brain is estimated to be between 10^{14} and 10^{18} connections! It is the universe within. This mind-boggling (pun intended) number of possibilities for human uniqueness lets us know that in all likelihood no two brain patterns would ever be exactly alike. Further, it is somehow this pattern that persists in a person over the course of a lifetime. The actual atoms in a given person's body change and are replaced over the course of years. The physical energy, matter, and atoms in my body right now are not the same as when I was a freshman in college. Through the normal operations of blood cell production, skin production (and loss), eating and digestion, we slowly swap one set of atoms for another. The continuity of my person is not dependent on the "stuff" that makes up my body at any given moment but the pattern that gets imposed on whatever energy-matter happens to be in my body at any given time.

As all parents swiftly experience, not only does each human child come into the world with a certain amount of pre-wired personality and demeanor, but such personal uniqueness continues to develop and evolve over a lifetime of experience as new information is received and processed, as various ideas and plans lead a person in a given direction. Both the genetic makeup of an individual human brain and the myriad ways that brain continues to wire itself (or get re-wired) result in a wholly unique pattern of conscious selfhood. This is why perhaps the most boring question to ask a parent of so-called "identical twins" is, "How in the world can you tell them apart?" The answer is that this is not even remotely difficult: no matter how much twins may look alike physically (and are DNA spot-on matches), most parents of twins testify that this is where the resemblance stops. This may also refute the idea that a clone of yourself would be a way to perpetuate your life indefinitely: a clone of your DNA would no more end up just *being* you all over again than identical twins are mere redundancies of one another. Unless science can find a way of precisely duplicating brain patterns and life experiences which can shape individuals on the order of 10^{18} number of possibilities, then it is clear that there will *never* be another you. (And only the most extreme of narcissists would regard that assertion as anything but good news.)

Perhaps it is just this personally unique pattern that defines the individual and which can be preserved, and in some sense be kept alive, by God, even as the re-location of that pattern one day in a renewed body could be seen as the essence of resurrection. But we're still not home yet in terms of defining whether this constitutes a "soul" in the sense of something capable of any form of conscious, disembodied existence. After all, the unique pattern that I have just described remains primarily a pattern of neural connections. Wondrous though the nearly limitless possibilities are for different patterns within any given brain, they remain nevertheless quite stubbornly *physical* in nature. No lump of gray matter, no neurons. No neurons, no connections among neurons. No connections among neurons, no unique pattern. No unique pattern, no person.

True enough. However, though invisible to any science that can investigate only the physically observable, there remains a mysterious sense of "beyondness" to all of this. There is a major component to human self-consciousness and thought that is ultimately not a matter of biology — or at least there are key features to human life that resist reduction to mere biology. The way new ideas can alter one's own mind (as well as the minds of those who receive the communication of such ideas from God or from other people) may well have an effect on biology despite not being strictly speaking biological in nature. For instance, neurologists say that when a child learns a new task — say, riding a bike without training wheels — there is a reason why, as the old adage has it, once you learn it, you never forget (barring disease or damage, of course). The reason is that what gets acquired in this new skill actually tends to re-wire the way the brain works — some new neural pathways and connections get added from among that staggering welter of interconnection possibilities I mentioned earlier. The brain changes and, in some way, the person changes, too.

Similar brain events/changes may occur through the impartation of many different kinds of information. This is quite a mysterious phenomenon. Apparently significant changes to a person (to personality, to outlook on life, to the actual functioning of a given brain) can occur without the person in question ever being touched. Nothing physical gets added to a brain under such conditions: no surgery makes neural insertions, no chemical from the outside gets ingested, no sonic beam or laser beam penetrates a person's cranium. Rather the sheer communication of invisible information — the passing along of a skill, of an idea, of a divine revelation — can have profound effects physically, mentally, spiritually, even biologically.

John Haught has written about the mysterious yet real role "information" plays in complex physical systems: "By 'information' I mean, in a broad and general sense, the overall ordering of entities — atoms, molecules, cells, genes, etc. — into intelligible forms or arrangements. . . . Though it is not physically separate, information is logically distinguishable from mass and energy. Information is quietly resident in nature, and in spite of being nonenergetic and nonmassive, it powerfully patterns subordinate natural elements and routines into hierarchically distinct domains."[1] Clearly Haught is reflecting a development in scientific theory that is highly mysterious and hard to define. Haught suggests that in evolution it is God who could plausibly be seen as the provider of the information that patterns brute matter into the kind of cosmos in which life is able to exist. The role of this invisible information hints at something beyond the sheerly physical which exercises a profound influence on the physical world. As Haught says of the role of information, "we are entering into one of . . . the great mysteries. We do not grasp it so much as it grasps us."[2]

Somehow something similar appears to happen within each human being, as the unique pattern of that individual is able to order the physical matter of the brain and body in such a way as to provide a continuity of personhood over the course of a lifetime. So although the formation of a personally unique pattern gets somehow built upon an undeniably physical foundation, there are influences on and operations of this pattern that cannot be traced down to some biological set of molecules or anything else that could be mounted onto a microscope slide or detected in a sample of brain tissue. Hence, if even on the strictly human level we are able to recognize a sphere of activity (information) that could also be described as "purely mental" or even as "spiritual," then how could we deny on the divine level of activity the possibility of God's being able to take hold of, expand on, realize, and even preserve human patterns of thought — that patterned essence of each human person — in some sense that is truly "alive" even if, for a time, disembodied?

That is, if even *while* we are undeniably physical and embodied beings we simultaneously move in and are influenced by non-biological realms (and are even in key ways constituted by such factors), then we cannot plausibly deny that God can and does also operate in such realms, both knowing who each person is in his/her uniqueness and being able to preserve that real essence after death and prior to resurrection. If our own mental events have a reality and a power that defy physical descriptions (and that apparently transcend the purely physical), then surely God's "mental events" would have a much thicker and more substantial reality to them when preserving each person's fascinatingly complex pattern. (Indeed, it could be alleged that *only* God would have the ability to grasp in its entirety even *one* full person, much less hosts of such complicated creatures.)

Hence what I am suggesting in this essay is that there is within the human person a high-order pattern of information that may well be where the essence of that person resides over and above the physical matter this information patterns. This pattern would not have existed without the physical body/brain from which it emerged, but once a conscious human being with such a unique pattern exists, there is more to that person than just physio-biological facets. This pattern and the information it contains and conveys are real. This "soul" has power and influence and, therefore, its own kind of reality despite its not being reducible to something that can be slid under a microscope or detected in a CAT scan. This soul is, in fact, *so* real as to have a substantial, ontological reality — what God holds within his divine mind after someone dies is not just the memory of the person but the *living* pattern, the actual essence whose reality, though originally rooted in the physical matter/brain where it had previously resided (and without which it had never before been visible), has by God's design become a living soul, which God can and will preserve until that time when it will once more have a new body to form and pattern in the resurrection of the dead.

The continuity between our present bodies and what Paul in 1 Corinthians 15 calls the "spiritual" body of the resurrection would not be a physical continuity any more than the continuity of my present body at the age of 65 will be a physical continuity with the body I had when I was 18, the matter and atoms within my body having been exchanged several times in those intervening years. Rather the continuity will be in the "soul" of the person as it resides within and emerges from that mysterious pattern of information that has the power to order matter into the essence of the person in question. What's more, I am suggesting that God's maintaining a given person's pattern in the divine mind/memory is a phenomenon of such thick and substantial reality as to constitute conscious existence "in Christ." If so, then, this could indeed be in line with the doctrine of the intermediate state.

Conclusion

On the old TV series "Star Trek," the "transporter" is how Captain Kirk and Mr. Spock got around. They would get "beamed" down from the starship Enterprise to the planet below. The premise of this fictional machine is that a computer was able to scan Captain Kirk's body, memorize every single speck of energy in that body (as well as every single connection and pattern within the body and brain of Kirk), translate the physical body into pure energy, beam it somewhere else like a radio signal, and then re-assemble the whole kit and kaboodle at the destination specified. Of course, scientists admit that it would be impossible ever to develop such a device. The amount of data in just one person could never be analyzed by, much less stored in, any computer. We are, each one of us, simply too complex.

The Christian faith claims that God, however, is able to maintain, store, and re-assemble your unique pattern and my unique pattern and everyone's unique pattern. If God cannot do that, then death is the end. If God can do that, then hope flourishes once again. Is it a miracle of staggering, mind-boggling complexity? Of course! That's why Christians call the first cosmic instance of this, Jesus' resurrection from the dead, "the grand miracle." Christians of all people are not casual about what happened to Jesus, nor about what we believe will one day happen for us all.

For now we mourn loved ones who have died, and we want to know that somehow they are still all right, still "with Christ," still in existence somehow. The thought of total non-existence, even for a short while, disturbs many people. After all, we remember our departed loved ones so well and so fondly; we see them so clearly, even still "hearing" their voices and laughs. But we are not the only ones who remember all that made those people the unique individuals we loved. God remembers them, too. And he has a plan. Easter.

12. *"Jesus, Remember Me"*

David Miles

Introduction

This project finds its inspiration in the last words spoken by a man about to die. They are the famous words that were uttered by the thief who was hanging on the cross beside the crucified Jesus. They are the last words, according to Luke's Gospel, spoken to Christ before his death. It is this final exchange between this dying man and Jesus Christ that, I believe, provides a unique window into one aspect of the nature of what it means to be a human being, and into the nature of the relationship between humanity and God.

> One of the criminals who were hanged there kept deriding him and saying, "Are you not the Messiah? Save yourself and us!" But the other

> rebuked him, saying, "Do you not fear God, since you are under the same sentence of condemnation? And we indeed have been condemned justly, for we are getting what we deserve for our deeds, but this man has done nothing wrong." Then he said, "Jesus, remember me when you come into your kingdom." (Luke 23:39-42)

It is in these last words of the dying thief that we hear a human longing that is expressed over and over in the biblical witness: the longing to be remembered by God. What does it say about the nature of the human beings that the human person longs to be remembered, and more specifically, to be remembered by God? To what extent is "memory" a part of being human? What does the human longing to be "remembered" and not "forgotten" say about theological anthropology? Can we speak of such a thing as "the memory of God"? And of what pastoral value, if any, is the use of such language as "being held in the memory of God"?

While it is not possible here to do a complete analysis of the theological, historical, and psychological aspects of "memory," this project will attempt an analysis of the concept of "memory" as found in the biblical witness. The focus here will be on how the words "remember" and "forget" function in Scripture, and how their use might reflect on the nature of humanity and the nature of God.

Remember and Do Not Forget

The English word *remember* arose in the fourteenth century, via the old French *remembrer*, from the late Latin *rememorari*. This comes from the Latin *memor*, "mindful," from which we get the English word *memory*. To "remember" has come to mean any of the following things: to recall something forgotten, to keep something in memory, to keep somebody in mind, to give someone a gift, or to commemorate something of someone. Conversely, to "forget" is to not remember, to leave behind, to neglect someone or something, to stop thinking about or fail to mention some one or something.

While one is hard pressed to find in the Bible a theoretical or psychological account of the nature of memory, the Scriptures are full of references to memory and remembering. The Hebrew verb *zkr* is found in the Qal conjugation 168 times in the Old Testament, meaning "to remember, recall, reflect on, or commemorate." It appears in the *niphal* (passive) conjugation, "to be remembered or invoked," and also in the *hiphal* (causative) conjugation, "to bring to remembrance, to mention or invoke." The definition of the verb gains further clarity because it is often paired with other verbs, most commonly in the negative with the verb for "forget," as in "remember, and do not forget." Such parallelism shows that *zākar* denotes the presence and acceptance of something in the mind.

While *zākar* frequently expresses thought of the past, the biblical notion of "remember" is not confined to memory of things past. The future can also be the subject of the intellectual activity expressed by *zākar*, as in Isaiah 47:7, where Babylon should have remembered its end, and a man should remember the coming "days of darkness" (Eccl. 11:8). In the New Testament, the Greek *mimnēskomai* also transcends recollection of things past, as things present (Col. 4:18) as well as things future (Heb. 11:22) can be remembered.

The family of words derived from the Hebrew root *zkr* has a prominent place in the faith of Israel. In Israel's memory, it keeps the meaning of the past alive, reflects on it, and puts it to use in the present. Unlike our typically one-dimensional notion of memory as primarily a mental recollection of the past, the act of "remembering" in the Bible is not simply that of recollection, but a combination of thinking and acting that brings the past into the present.

One does not have to read far into the Old Testament to find that "remembering" is one of the indispensable elements of God's covenant with the people of Israel. At the outset of the giving of the law, the people are repeatedly to "*Remember* that you were a slave in the land of Egypt, and the Lord your God brought you out from there with a mighty hand and an outstretched arm" (Deut. 5:15). When the people are in exile they are encouraged to "*Remember* the Lord in a distant land, and let Jerusalem come into your mind" (Jer. 51:50). Remembering God's past dealings with Israel brings knowledge and power over history (Isa. 46:8-9), and memory of God's faithfulness is essential for Israel's continued loyalty to God (Deut. 6:20-25; 8:1-2).

While the occurrence of human remembering is not as extensive in the New Testament, it is a no less central theme. The letters of Paul call upon the believers in the churches to remember the tradition he first gave to them, which he had received from others or the Lord Jesus himself (esp. 1 Cor. 15:1). Other epistles emphasize the centrality of remembering in the life of faith (esp. Eph. 2:11; 2 Thess. 2:5; 2 Tim. 2:8; 2 Pet. 3:2). However, for Christians throughout the ages, the most important mention of remembering is in the accounts of the Last Supper where we are told to "do this in remembrance of me."

Can We Even Speak of "The Memory of God"?

While it is clear from the biblical witness that human memory is of central importance in Israel's faith and the faith of the church, the striking thing about the role of memory in the covenant relationship with God (Old or New) is that the remembering always goes both ways. Just as the people are called to remember, there is also an expectation that God will "remember" too.

The first question that immediately arises from this idea relates to the appropriateness of using anthropomorphic terms such as "remember" and "forget" to speak of God. Language of memory is, by definition, language that presupposes time. To say that one "remembers" or "forgets" presupposes the past, present, and future. To remember or to forget someone requires that this one was known at a previous point in time. Likewise, the promise to remember or the possibility of forgetting requires the future tense. Therefore, the attempt to apply anthropomorphic language of memory directly to God would be a mistake if we believe that God transcends time and is not strictly bound by time as are human beings. In other words, if we are going to say that "God remembers," as with all theological language, we must acknowledge that we do not mean by that precisely the same thing as when we say "we remember."

There remain, however, abundant references to the memory of God in the biblical witness, as well as a constant longing expressed by human beings to be remembered by God. While God may not exist solely "in time," the biblical references to the memory of God point to the fact that God chooses to participate "in time" with humanity. Given that we cannot step out of time to speak of either the nature of God or our own nature, the language of "memory" remains a valuable lens through which we focus on theological anthropology, the nature of the human being in relation to reality of God.

The Longing to Be Remembered in Death

The request by the thief to be remembered when Jesus "comes into his kingdom" is made from within time. The thief makes the request from within his earthly life, albeit quickly nearing its end. But his request is for something that transcends his earthly life. He knows nothing of what to expect in death, but he believes that the one dying next to him will "enter into his kingdom." The hope expressed by the thief upon the cross does not refer to any particular notion of the afterlife per se. Rather, it is simply the hope that the one dying next to him might be able to carry the memory of him into the unknown beyond this life, that his life might be somehow held in the memory of God.

As experiences of alienation, suffering, and loss are often experienced as feeling "forgotten" by God, this becomes most clear when the subject turns to death. In a number of places throughout Scripture, death itself is described as the place where one is forgotten. Being remembered is juxtaposed with being forgotten as death is often spoken of as the time, place, or experience of being forgotten by God, as well as the place where one forgets.

> Turn, O LORD, save my life; deliver me for the sake of your steadfast love. For in death there is no remembrance of you; in Sheol who can give you praise? (Psalm 6:4-5)

> I am counted among those who go down to the Pit; I am like those who have no help, like those forsaken among the dead, like the slain that lie in the grave, like those whom you *remember* no more, for they are cut off from your hand. . . .
>
> Do you work wonders for the dead? Do the shades rise up to praise you? Is your steadfast love declared in the grave, or your faithfulness in Abaddon? Are your wonders known in the darkness, or your saving help in the land of *forgetfulness?* (Psalm 88:4-5, 10-12)

> The people of long ago are not remembered, nor will there be any *remembrance* of people yet to come by those who come after them. . . . For there is no enduring *remembrance* of the wise or of fools, seeing that in the days to come all will have been long *forgotten.* How can the wise die just like fools? (Ecclesiastes 1:11; 2:16)

While the experience of feeling "forgotten" is one of the most tragic things we can experience in life, that same feeling is used to express the fear of what awaits us beyond this life. It is from this most primal fear that the longing comes to be remembered by God beyond this life, to be held in God's memory on the other side.

The Hope of the Memory of God

The biblical witness speaks of humanity being held in the memory of God beyond this life. The first hints come, however, not only in death, but also before we are born.

> For it was you who formed my inward parts; you knit me together in my mother's womb. I praise you, for I am fearfully and wonderfully made. Wonderful are your works; that I know very well. My frame was not hidden from you, when I was being made in secret, intricately woven in the depths of the earth. Your eyes beheld my unformed substance. In your book were written all the days that were formed for me, when none of them as yet existed. (Psalm 139:13-16)

> Now the word of the LORD came to me, saying, "Before I formed you in the womb I knew you, and before you were born I consecrated you; I appointed you a prophet to the nations." (Jeremiah 1:4-5)

However poetic this may be, the image derived from the biblical witness affirms that God knows human beings before anyone else knows them.

But what about after this life? Is there hope of being held in the memory of God after one's life is over? This brings us back, of course, to the thief hanging on the cross next to Jesus. He makes his request of Jesus, but what will the reply be?

> Then he said, "Jesus, *remember* me when you come into your kingdom." He replied, "Truly I tell you, today you will be with me in Paradise." (Luke 23:42-43)

What is so interesting about the response of Jesus to the thief dying next to him is that, while the request of the thief is made from within time, Jesus gives him an answer that uses the language of time to speak of something that transcends time. Even though the "day" is nearly over for these two crucified men, Jesus assures him that "today" the thief will be with him in paradise.

It is in this moment, just before these two men die, that time and eternity intersect in an interesting way. The thief is longing for something beyond this life, to be held in the memory of God. He makes this request from within time, and the answer is given back to him in terms of time. It is an answer that transcends time, but is given to him in terms that he can understand while still in this life. It is also a hope that may have the power to transform this life, knowing that we will always be held in the memory of God.

The Unique Nature of God's Memory

Reflecting on the work of Bernard Lonergan, Frederick Crowe presents an interesting way of thinking about the eternity of God and the nature of the risen Christ.[3] His proposal revolves around the way Lonergan employs the simple word "is." He raises the same question that a recent President made famous: "It all depends what your definition of 'is' is." Lonergan says that one can think of "is" in contrast to "was" and "will be." But there is also a second way, he proposes, in which "is" is not contrasted with "was" and "will be" but rather finds a common element in all three. He speaks of this as a definition that does not include a reference to time, but is rather the radical meaning of "is."

He proposes a four-dimensional universe in which past, present, and future are not divided off from one another, but are all part of one universe of being. While there is no appropriate word in English to speak of this, Lonergan, writing in Latin, used the word *simul.* God is simul with all things that are in the universe of being. While it is easy to assert that God is present to all creation, Lonergan goes on to ask what this might mean for us:

> To answer that, let us set aside for a moment, the notions of "when" and "simul" and think of the presence of all things to God as their reality. Am I more real than my grandparents who are dead? Well, put the question another way: Am I more present to God than they are? And

add the further question: Are they present to God only in memory or in their reality?[4]

This idea suggests that to speak of "the memory of God" is to say something more than when we speak of human remembering. To say that God remembers is not simply to affirm that God recollects something from the past, but that something is fully present, fully real in the universe of God's being. Given that we speak of such things from within the confines of time, the best way we have to speak of this is that "God remembers."

"All Are One in Thee for All Are Thine"

There is an interesting and cryptic exchange between Jesus and some of the Sadducees found in chapter 20 of Luke's Gospel. It appears that these Sadducees, who do not believe in the resurrection of the dead, are trying to tie up Jesus in a theological straightjacket with a complicated question about a hypothetical woman who marries seven brothers, one after the next, who keep dying. "In the resurrection, therefore, whose wife will the woman be, for the seven had married her?" (Luke 20:33). Jesus responds in the following way:

> Those who belong to this age marry and are given in marriage; but those who are considered worthy of a place in that age and in the resurrection from the dead neither marry nor are given in marriage. Indeed they cannot die anymore, because they are like angels and are children of God, being children of the resurrection. And the fact that the dead are raised Moses himself showed, in the story about the bush, where he speaks of the Lord as the God of Abraham, the God of Isaac, and the God of Jacob. Now he is God not of the dead, but of the living; for to him all of them are alive.

Most mythology throughout the ages pictures a great river, chasm, or some other impassable divide between the living and the dead. Yet the answer that Jesus gives the Sadducees provides an image of the living and the dead all being fully present to the being of God. To say that God is "the God of the living, not the dead," is to say that those whom we speak of in the past tense are all in the "present tense" for God. This text supports an image of all humanity held together in the life of God, just as the great hymn "For All the Saints" states, "Yet all are one in Thee for all are Thine."

The Danger of Speaking of "The Memory of God"

One danger of speaking of being held in the memory of God is losing the human subject in the process (so to speak), as process theologians have come dangerously close to doing. If we speak of eternal life as "being held in God's memory," it is easy to lose track of the human subject as something "other" than God, as God's memory may become all that really matters. This is a clear danger of using this language to speak of human hope.

Robert Jenson has made an interesting proposal in response to this concern. He affirms that even though our death is simply our non-existence, this is not a sheer occurrence of nothingness, because the whole of our experience is preserved in the memory of God. However, Jenson goes on to say,

> That proposal does not work if we leave the whole matter where it is usually left. That is to say, if we leave out the doctrine of the Trinity. But the matter works out very differently if the doctrine of the Trinity is taken into account.[5]

He explains that through all the centuries of Christian reflection the idea of our existence as an actual thing other than God, as those whose consciousness is finite, is "enabled within the otherness of the Son from the Father."[6] The otherness of the Son from the Father is most clearly seen in the Son's death, in the cry "My God, my God, why hast thou forsaken me?" particularly. And it is the "otherness" of the Son from the Father that allows there to be "other things" than God. Just as the death of Christ is integral to the otherness of the Son, our death is integral to that relationship within which "we are" in the first place.

> The vanishing of being belongs to that relation between the Father and the Son that is the very life of God; belongs to the life that grounds all life. The mind of God within which I am remembered is the reasoning

> and the will loved out between the Father and the Son in the Spirit. And to be remembered *there* is to live more fully than we can otherwise conceivably imagine.[7]

This, of course, brings even greater significance to the words "*Jesus*, remember me. . . ." For to be held in the memory of God does not mean that, upon death, our self is merely subsumed into the vast, all-encompassing being of God, like so many drops of water vanishing into the ocean. No, it is precisely within the relationship between the "Jesus" to whom we call out and the Father to whom he has gone that our distinct self is "remembered."

Concluding Thoughts

Memory itself is central to what it means to be human. This becomes painfully clear from people who suffer from Alzheimer's disease. Even those closest to them will admit that when Alzheimer's patients lose their memory, they are no longer completely "themselves." Something that is basic to their humanity is lost. Now, this certainly does not mean that they are no longer human. It does reflect, however, how significant a role memory plays in what makes us a human being.

And yet we may receive a strange glimpse of grace from the tragedy of those who lose their ability to remember. While we may speak of God's covenants with us as "remembering that goes both ways," Alzheimer's patients provide the powerful reminder of a central hope of the Christian faith: ultimately, our lives rest not on our ability to remember God, but on God's ability to remember us. Even when we are not longer able to remember, we are still held in the memory of God.

While the longing to be remembered by God may be only one thin slice of the totality of what it means to be a human being, I believe that it reflects a dimension of human nature that points beyond life that is bound by time. It seems to suggest that there is some part of the human that longs for something eternal. We have to ask, "Why else would one want to be remembered?"

So many of the ways in which we might long to be remembered will ultimately be forgotten. Even the memories our loved ones have of us begin to fade. Even the books we write will yellow with time. Even great buildings built with our names on them will someday crumble. Yet the fact that human beings express this longing to be remembered by God suggests that there may be, in each of us, a dimension of ourselves that has the capacity to transcend time, the memory of something eternal.

13. The Nature of the Soul

J. Harold McKeithen Jr.

> What is the nature of the individual person? . . . Perhaps there will someday emerge an understanding of the human so overwhelmingly persuasive that only cranks will dissent. For the foreseeable future, however, anyone reflecting on this question will have to make some crucial choices, assumptions or acts of faith. At what might be called the relatively unreflective level, "you picks your horses and bets your money" and let it go at that. Some will accept without question that we are merely what can be seen and touched, weighed and measured; others who insist that we are more than our bodies will simply *assert* that this "more" is spirit or soul. . . . Both views . . . can be broadly reduced to two classical modes: namely, materialism and dualism. . . . There are numerous . . . efforts to devise a doctrine of the self that escapes both classical materialism and classical dualism. These efforts, in my opinion, offer the richest possibilities for an adequate doctrine of the self.[8]

I share this opinion expressed by Eugene Fontinell and will explore the kind of doctrine that moves in the direction he indicates. I will first offer a critique of the scientific materialism of Edward O. Wilson and will then explore three views that seek to do justice to both the materialist and non-materialist aspects of human being: the non-reductive physicalism of Nancey Murphy and Warren Brown, the developmentalism of John Hick, and the pragmatism of William James. I will then draw some conclusions from these explorations. Throughout, I will be using the terms *mind, soul,* and *self* interchangeably.

The Scientific Materialism of Edward O. Wilson

A powerful case can be made for scientific materialism, and Edward O. Wilson makes that case in his 1978 book, *On Human Nature.* At the outset, he summarizes his position this way:

> Species may have vast potential for material and mental progress but they lack any immanent purpose or guidance from agents beyond their immediate environment or even an evolutionary goal toward which their molecular architecture automatically steers them. I believe that the human mind is constructed in a way that locks it inside this fundamental constraint and forces it to make choices with a purely biological instrument. If the brain evolved by natural selection, even the capacities to select particular esthetic judgments and religious beliefs must have arisen by the same mechanistic process.[9]

Wilson describes convincingly how natural selection and neurobiological processes combine to produce and govern all aspects of human being, which he discusses in the categories of "heredity, development, emergence, aggression, sex, altruism and religion."

With respect to religion, he says that "the mental processes of religious belief . . . represent programmed predispositions whose self-sufficient components were incorporated into the neural apparatus of the brain by thousands of generations of genetic evolution."[10] He says that Isaac Newton regarded two texts as having been given by God to humankind, the book of nature and the book of scriptures, and that science has now brought us to a point where God has been pushed "to somewhere below the subatomic particles or beyond the farthest visible galaxy."[11]

The relentless determinism of Wilson's data and arguments becomes increasingly oppressive and nihilistic in spite of the confident and spirited tenor of his presentation. I believe that he is able to maintain that spirit only because he does not really believe what he is saying. In the last chapter of his book, he writes the following statements that contain clauses at radical variance with his argument. I have italicized those clauses. Referring to those genetically determined religious beliefs, he says,

> I suggest that scientific materialism must accommodate them on two levels: as a scientific puzzle of great complexity and interest, and as a

> source of energies *that can be shifted in new directions* when scientific materialism itself is accepted as the more powerful mythology. . . . There is reason to entertain the view that the culture of each society travels along one or the other of a set of evolutionary trajectories whose full array is constrained by the genetic rules of human nature. . . . As our knowledge of human nature grows, *and we start to elect a system of values* on a more objective basis, and our minds at last *align with our hearts,* the set of trajectories will narrow still more. . . . As the social sciences mature into predictive disciplines, *the permissible trajectories* will not only diminish in number but our descendants will be able to sight farther along them.[12]

The only way in which energies could be "shifted" and values could be "elected" and trajectories could be "permitted" would be by a mind or soul or self free of the determinism that he claims is total and unqualified.

This leads to a more comprehensive critique of the theory of scientific materialism. I draw here upon the work of John Hick in his book *Death and Eternal Life,*[13] and that of Paul Badham in his book *Christian Beliefs About Life After Death.*[14] Both Hick and Badham take scientific materialism very seriously and believe, in fact, that heredity and environment account for the entire range of a person's character traits. What they reject is reduction of human being to physical properties and processes.

Badham, in particular, argues persuasively that materialism is a "self-refuting theory."[15] He summarizes his argument this way:

> We can only check the validity of our own reasons if we are free agents. A computer can make calculations, check figures, and prove theorems, but it cannot check the validity of its own programming. And if we too are programmed we cannot check the validity of our own theories of knowledge. If our minds are physically determined then we have no way of deciding between the merits of different theories of knowledge, for any conclusions we might come to would merely indicate the nature of our brain's programming and not whether its conclusions were true or false. . . . Physical determinism falls prey to the same criticism as any other determinist system, namely that if it could apparently be proved true it would, in that proving, be falsified.[16]

Badham goes on to quote J. R. Lucas, who observed, "The Marxist who says that all ideologies have no independent validity and merely reflect the class interests of those who hold them can be told that in that case his Marxist views merely express the economic interests of his class, and have no more claim to be adjudged true or valid than any other views."[17]

A second criticism raised by Badham is that numerous scientists working in the fields of genetics and neurophysiology flatly reject the conclusions reached by scientists such as Edward Wilson. Quoting Sir John Eccles, winner of a Nobel Prize in 1963 for his work on the brain, he says, "the brain is just the sort of machine a ghost could operate." And he quotes an eminent physician, Dr. Wilder Penfield, as saying, "Can we visualize a spiritual element . . . capable of controlling this mechanism? When a patient is asked about the movement which he carries out as a result of cortical stimulation, he is never in any doubt about it. He knows that there is a difference between automatic action and voluntary action. He would agree that something else finds its dwelling place between the sensory complex and the motor mechanism, that there is a switchboard operator as well as a switchboard."[18] This, of course, is what Edward Wilson seemed to be allowing, in spite of himself, in the telling clauses I quoted earlier.

A third critique that both Badham and Hick level at so-called scientific materialism is that it is not scientific enough, in that it ignores data that should not be ignored. Both of them take seriously the phenomena of mental telepathy and the scientific evidence adduced especially by J. B. Rhine at the Parapsychology Institute at Duke University and by L. A. Vasiliev at the Leningrad Institute for Brain Research. Both Badham and Hick are in agreement with Keith Campbell, who writes,

> Parapsychological phenomena, by definition, demonstrate capacities of mind which exceed any capacities of brain. The brain is receptive only to information which arrives by neural pathways, and so is confined to perception by way of the senses. If some people can learn more about distant, hidden, or future fact than memory and inference from sense perception can teach them, then their minds are just not brains. . . . If even a single example of para-normal phenomena is genuine. . . . Materialism is false.[19]

A fourth criticism Badham and Hick level at scientific materialism is that it is unscientific in its *a priori* rejection of the mystical experience of countless human beings whose lives have been profoundly and permanently changed by a personal encounter with a transcendent reality beyond themselves. To maintain that such occurrences cannot be what they clearly seem to be and what they are perceived to be because they do not fit into the theory of scientific materialism does in fact appear arbitrary and unscientific.

The Non-reductive Physicalism of Nancey Murphy and Warren Brown

Turn now from a consideration of scientific materialism to a consideration of a theory of the relationship of body and mind that attempts to do justice to both the insights of materialism and idealism. Consider the theory of "non-reductive physicalism."

Non-reductive physicalism, as defined by Nancey Murphy, holds that "the person is a physical organism whose complex functioning, both in society and in relation to God, gives rise to 'higher' human capacities such as morality and spirituality."[20] In this view, "soul" is not a word that describes an entity or substance that distinguishes human beings; it is a word that describes distinguishing capacities and functions.

More specifically, in the view of Warren Brown, soul is the capacity for and experience of relatedness to the self, to others, and to God; and this capacity for relatedness is "an emergent property of certain cognitive abilities."[21] The abilities he identifies and analyzes are the capacities for

1. *Language:* the capacity to communicate a potentially infinite number of propositions; to relate regarding complex, abstract ideas, as well as about the past and future.
2. *A theory of mind:* an ability to consider the most likely thoughts and feelings of another person.
3. *Episodic memory:* a conscious historical memory of events, persons, times, and places (i.e., more than memory for actions and their consequences).
4. *Conscious top-down agency:* conscious mental control of behavior;

the ability to modulate ongoing behavior in relationship to the conscious process of decision making.

5. *Future orientation:* the ability to run mental scenarios of the future implications of behaviors and events.
6. *Emotional modulation:* a capacity for empathy that serves to guide ongoing behavior and decision making.

The heart of Brown's proposal is that, while these capacities emerge from lower-level abilities upon which they are dependent, they "cannot be understood by close scrutiny of the lower abilities."[22] In other words, the whole is more than the sum of its parts. In addition, the functioning of this "whole" has "a downward causative influence on the ongoing and future activity of the lower-level processes (i.e., top-down causation)."[23] Brown sums up his thoughts this way:

> The soulful aspects of human experience are engendered by the experiences of *personal relatedness.* This relatedness, in turn, is an emergent property of certain critical *human cognitive capacities.* Just as the properties of soul presumed by Jewish and Christian Scripture emerge from personal relatedness, so also personal relatedness emerges from the operation of the incredibly enhanced mental powers of humans. In the plan and design of God, the richness and depth of human interpersonal relatedness was made possible by an evolutionary explosion of our mental capacities.[24]

There is an impressive correspondence between these higher capacities identified by Brown and the picture of human being at its best that we see in the Bible. To give but a few examples:

1. Nothing is more fundamental to human being than *language.* It is by speech that God brings human being into existence. It is by speech that human beings relate meaningfully to God and to each other.
2. If *theory of mind* is the capacity accurately to attribute mental states to others, Psalm 139 is a place where a writer manifests that capacity in very familiar words,

> O Lord, thou hast searched me and known me!
> Thou knowest when I sit down and when I rise up;

> Thou discernest my thoughts from afar.
> Even before a word is on my tongue,
> Lo, O Lord, thou knowest it altogether.

3. A capacity for *episodic memory* is essential to the very life of Israel and of the church. In Israel's case, it is the memory and rehearsal of God's "mighty acts" in her history (see the credo in Deuteronomy 26:5-11). In the church's case, it is also the memory and rehearsal of God's acts in the life, death, and resurrection of Jesus (see Peter's sermon in Acts 2).
4. While human existence in the Bible is subject always to God's purpose, it is also invested with a capacity for self-determination — that is, with a capacity for *top-down agency.* Nowhere is this better expressed than in the exhortation of the Apostle Paul in Philippians 2:12-13, "Work out your own salvation with fear and trembling, for God is at work in you, both to will and to work for his good pleasure."
5. In the Bible, the capacity for *future orientation,* the ability to imagine the future consequences of present behavior, is basic to human being. One can live purposefully and sacrificially only when one can imagine the results of such living. In Philippians 3, Paul writes, "I count everything as loss because of the surpassing worth of knowing Christ Jesus my Lord. For his sake I have suffered the loss of all things, and count them as refuse, in order that I may gain Christ and be found in him."
6. The capacity for *emotional responsiveness* not only sets human beings apart from other animals; it sets whole human beings apart from defective ones, such as psychopaths. In the Bible, a whole person is one who can rejoice with those who rejoice and weep with those who weep (Romans 12:15).

The capacities for relationship that, according to non-reductive physicalism, define the soul are very resonant with those capacities that make for true human being in the Bible. And there is no dichotomy between the physical and the non-physical; they are interdependent.

This idea of the self or soul progressing through this mortal life and through a postmortem life until it reaches the full potential God intended is at radical variance with the traditional, orthodox theology in which I have been reared and to which I have been committed. It is also at variance with the practical theology with which I operate, especially with my affirmation that the souls or selves of believers are, at their death, joined with all the saints who have died and who live with God in heaven. My task now is to wrestle with the question of whether my emerging views can be reconciled with my long-held views and, if so, how?

CHAPTER V

Reconciled in Christ

Introduction

The Christian church is confessed to be the people of God who are called, gathered, enlightened, and sent into the world by the Word of God. Whether it is also described in such other biblical images as the communion of saints or as members of the body of Christ, the stress is always on the church's corporate character at the heart of the New Testament's ecclesial anthropology. You cannot be a Christian alone. The Holy Spirit unites around the risen Christ a public community ("a chosen race, a royal priesthood, a holy nation, God's own people," 1 Peter 2:9), in order to proclaim God's "mighty acts" in word and deed, joyfully, faithfully, and hopefully. Christian anthropology is fulfilled when co-created persons are also reconciled and redeemed together in the adoration and service of the Triune God.

Richard L. Floyd explores what it means to be human in response to God's salvific act in Christ, as expressed in the congregational hymns of Isaac Watts. In his more than 750 hymn texts, this famed Reformed Christian called the faithful to a God-centered ministry of praise and obedience. The author organizes this treasure of gracious and generous orthodoxy around major foci of Christian anthropology:

1. the *created* self refers to the social and natural relationships within which the self lives and is shaped;
2. the *sinful* self refers to the reality that one is not what God intends one to be;

3. the *forsaken* self is the situation in which human persons find themselves without God;
4. the *forgiven and justified* self refers to the human results of God's atoning love in the death of Jesus Christ;
5. the *ecclesial* self refers to the process of sanctification that takes place within the life of Christ's church;
6. the *eschatological* self refers to the realization that "our life is hidden with Christ in God" (Colossians 3:3), the promised self that is now only in promise; and finally
7. the *worshipful* self, which finds its true life within a community that is centered in the cross and resurrection of Jesus Christ as the climax and center of the Christian story revealed in Holy Scripture.

J. Barry Vaughn explores the dialectic of "spirit and flesh" in baptism. His focus is on how the Christian tradition, as embodied in the church's earliest baptismal liturgies, speaks to us about human nature in our old and new creations. Employing a Johannine perspective on Christian anthropology (as created finitude rather than rebellious sin), he lauds the capacity of flesh and matter as the bearer of divine grace. The Fathers of the early church taught the "interpenetration and inseparability of the spiritual and the physical" in the church's celebration of the sacraments, preeminently in the water of baptism that serves as a vehicle of the Spirit's regeneration. Surveyed are the coherent teachings of Tertullian, Chrysostom, Theodore, Ambrose, Augustine, and Hippolytus, in explicating the "awe-inspiring rites of initiation" within the early Christian communities. As water and Spirit encompass the candidate's entire body, baptism is interpreted by the Patristic teachers holistically as a type of Christ's death and resurrection; the anointings for exorcism and the gift of the Spirit; the enlightenment from spiritual darkness; the initial stage of lifelong human divinization; the putting-off of one's demonic old nature and the putting-on of a righteous new one; and one's gracious entry into the bread and wine fellowship of a Eucharistic community dedicated to the glory of the Triune God.

For F. Harry Daniel, "rootedness" is a profound biblical image for the Christian community's ecclesial nature and homiletical renewal. Roots go far deeper than institutionalism and professionalism. Unless pastor-theologians are rooted in proclaiming the Christ-event, God's people have no hope of themselves being rooted solidly in the harvest of those who have been set apart for life eternal. Two biblical texts that help to explore the anthropological implications of rootedness are the parable of the tares in Matthew 13:24-30 and the prayer in Ephesians 3:14-21. Both depend upon faithful hearing, and assume that part of what it means to be a human being in history is to be addressed by another with a message requiring a response. Also for both, being "rooted" means obeying Jesus' words (Matthew) or being grounded in love (Ephesians). To be rightly rooted is to share in the God-given capacity for lifelong growth in the gracious favor of the Triune God.

For current application, the author then goes on to posit ten theses that seek to draw out the homiletical implications for all Christian preaching that is itself rooted in the anthropological world of these two New Testament texts. Both aim at rooting the rootless in the church for a good life that "bears good fruit" (Matthew 7:17).

14. *The Worshiping Self*

Richard L. Floyd

What does it mean to be human in response to the God with a human face who died on the cross for our justification? I propose to explore this question in conversation with the theological anthropology of Isaac Watts as expressed in some of his more than 750 hymn texts.

Why look at the hymns of Isaac Watts for a study in theological anthropology? Let me answer that in two parts: Why hymns? And why Watts?

Why Hymns?

There are several good reasons to look at hymns. Since Watts's time hymns have been a salient feature of Reformed worship, something Watts himself had no small part in bringing about. In hymn singing, the worshiping self experiences transcendence as one among many within a congregation. There, in worship, God "the other" is addressed by the singer, not in isolation, but as one voice among many others. The hymn singer uses the body as well as the intellect in an integrated act of worship engaging the whole self. Hymn singing also roots the worshiping self within the life of the congregation among whom the singer works and plays, rejoices and weeps. Since the congregation is the local embodiment of the church catholic (what P. T. Forsyth called "the great church"), the hymn singer is part not only of the congregation physically present, but also of the great congregation, both the ecumenical church in its geographical breadth and the communion of saints in its temporal length across ages and generations. Additionally, the hymn is a repository of the tradition of the great church, and the faithful learn scripture and doctrine from singing as much as they do from sermons and catechesis. Finally, and most significantly, the singer of hymns not only addresses God, but is at the same time addressed by God, so that hymn singing becomes an event of grace. The singer is addressed as a forgiven and justified sinner, and it is often in the singing of the hymns that the worshiping self is able to experience the grace of justification and respond with faith and obedience.

Why Watts?

But why Isaac Watts? In the first place, he is the most significant contributor to English hymnody, and his hymns, many of which are still sung today, are a rich field. Secondly, because his hymns were written before the coming of the arid rationalism of the eighteenth century, they retain a closeness to scripture and a doctrinal orthodoxy that, for the most part, transcends its historical context. His Reformed theology is not the unattractive rigid Calvinist scholasticism that has given Calvinism a bad name, but the aristocratic Puritanism of the years following the Restoration. If it is orthodoxy, it is, as Hans Frei once hoped for, a generous orthodoxy, at least for its day.

It is not just any hymns I want to be in conversation with, but those that express the central truth of the Christian faith: justification by God through the death of Jesus Christ. In other words, I want to approach anthropology through Christology and, more specifically, soteriology. Watts keeps Christ "and him crucified" (1 Corinthians 1:23) firmly in view as he writes his hymns: "Christ and his cross is all our theme . . ." (Book 1, Hymn 119, v 1).

Watts is wise, as well, about human beings as those who stand at the foot of the cross, and he knows that the worshiping self is the true self in ways that are lost to modernity, if we understand the chief characteristic of modernity to be the conviction that God is of no importance for how human beings are understood. Finally, there is a generosity and grace about Watts's hymns that belie their Calvinist core. If Watts never shied away from the realities of human sin — and he didn't — it was the reality of grace that shines through so many of his hymns, calling the Christian to a life of obedience and praise. As he expressed in his greatest hymn:

> Were the whole realm of nature mine,
> That were a present far too small;
> Love so amazing, so divine,
> Demands my soul, my life, my all.
>
> ("When I Survey the Wondrous Cross")

The texts used here come from two of Watts's collections: *The Psalms of David Imitated in the Language of the New Testament* of 1719, and *Hymns and Spiritual Songs* of 1707. The former collection is comprised of Watts's paraphrases of Scripture, viewed, as the title makes clear, through the lens of the New Testament. Many of them are explicitly Christological. This was a radical departure from the way the psalms were used in the Reformed worship of their day, and may be somewhat startling to those in our day who are committed to the current fashion of calling the Old Testament the Hebrew Bible (which it isn't, in either book order or literary history). Watts was right, in my view, that the church must always read the Old and New Testaments in light of the central truth of Jesus Christ and his cross. The latter collection is comprised of three books: the first composed from the scriptures, the second composed of divine subjects, and the third prepared for the Lord's Supper. Where I quote Watts I simply name either the book number and the hymn number or, in the case of the psalms, the psalm number. Sometimes he wrote more than one hymn to a psalm text, but I have not distinguished between these in my notation. Where I have quoted the Bible I have used the King James Version unless otherwise noted, since this was the Bible of Isaac Watts.

My approach here is neither historical nor critical. I am using Watts's words as illustrative of a particular theological anthropology. I make no claim to accurately mirror Watts's own anthropology, although I hope to capture the best of his gracious impulses. I want to distance myself from certain features of his thought, particularly a polemic against Roman Catholicism, a strong sense of the British nation as chosen by God to bring the gospel to the heathen, and a doctrine of double predestination that betrays his own sense of the scope of the work of Christ. In these particulars he demonstrates that he was a man of his age. We should beware of holding historical figures to the canons of twenty-first-century sensibilities, but at the same time we must be forthright where we disagree with them. I have no doubt that if Watts were living today, his own deep commitments to Christ and his church would move him to embrace a catholicity not imagined in his day. It is my hope that the present work will make Isaac Watts's rich contribution to Christian hymnody more widely available and contribute to an ecumenical Christian understanding of the human self that is truly catholic, truly evangelical, and truly Reformed.

What Is a self?

Lord, what is man, or all his race
  Who dwells so far below,
That thou shouldst visit him with grace,
  And love his nature so? (Psalm 8)

The psalmist's question is ours here: What is a human self, the "I" who stands in awe and wonder before the works of God? Like the psalmist, I want to ask it as a question understood in relationship with God as well as with other persons. This way of proceeding conveys my conviction that the human self cannot be rightly understood by itself apart from its relationship to God and others. That a highly individualized and atomistic self is a feature of much modern thinking about the human person means that the argument I press here is a critique of such approaches. The biblical and Christian understanding of a person offers a more adequate way to view the self.

Alistair McFadyen offers a useful theory of the self as understood biblically in his book *The Call to Personhood*. He puts forth a description of humanity, understood as created in the image of the Triune God and redeemed through God's address in Jesus Christ. This requires a relational understanding of human beings, in keeping with the relational character of the Triune God.

The principal features of McFadyen's understanding of the human self are thus: the identities of both humankind as a whole and individual persons are to be construed in terms of their response to God and others; identity denotes the way one enters into relations and is for others; this identity is derived from one's previous relations, by how one has been addressed by and responded to others; a person is a subject of communication, an "I" before the "I" of others; personhood is fostered through being addressed, through relations which take dialogical form.[1]

McFadyen's theological anthropology is very close to what I want to call "the worshiping self," the one who both addresses and is addressed. McFadyen's basic conception of a person is both dialogical (formed through social interaction) and dialectical (never coming to rest in final unity, since one is never removed from relation).[2] For McFadyen persons are centers or subjects of communication, but only so through their relations to others. So they are centered beings, but only in a personal way through relations with other personal centers. To conceive of persons in such a dialogical and dialectical manner makes it impossible to think of the human being as having a clearly defined center or foundation. The "I" of the human self is who it is only by virtue of its relations with other "I"'s, and for the worshiping self the decisive relationship is with the "I" of the God who addresses. There are vibrant Biblical resonances in this way of speaking; one thinks especially of Moses being addressed from the burning bush by the divine "I Am" (Exodus 3:14) and its counterpart in the Gospels, particularly in John, where Jesus is revealed as Messiah in a series of "I am" statements.

The worshiping self as I see it has these seven facets to it. (1) *The created self* refers to the whole network of social relationships in which the self lives and which shape it so decisively for both good and ill: family, voluntary associations, governmental and corporate structures, media and advertising, and the whole constellation of what the New Testament calls the principalities and powers of this age. In addition we must consider the self's relationship to the created world of nature and the global habitat, which is so interconnected with the social world. (2) The self is perennially and persistently not what God intends it to be, so one must understand *the self as sinner.* (3) *The forsaken self* is the actual condition in which human beings find themselves without God, which is the normative condition of the human being in modernity, defined as the world understood with no, or little, place for God. (4) Since the fallen and forsaken self, with its broken relationships with God and others, and indeed with the whole created order, can be healed only from God's side, we must keep in view God's act of atoning love in the death of Jesus Christ, and consider *the forgiven and justified self* that results from this act. (5) The forgiven self is also the self in Christ, turning toward God in response to his grace as plants turn toward the light of the sun. This process of sanctification is not an isolated and individual process, but takes place within the life of Christ's church. Therefore, as part of the social world, but having a special role for the self, is the church, the body of Christ, and so we must consider *the ecclesial self.* (6) Finally, since "our life is hidden with Christ in God," we must consider *the eschatological self,* the promised self who will be in actuality what it is now only in promise, as the fullness of God's act in Jesus Christ is actualized.

These facets roughly correspond to the main features of the Christian story: (1) Creation, (2) and (3) Fall, (4) Salvation (justification), (5) Covenant (Israel and the church), and (6) Consummation (the last things). Since the self as I understand it is always a "storied" self, we will explore its meaning within the larger story of God, the God who addresses and is addressed by (7) *the worshiping self.* This narrative approach wants to understand human selfhood as finding its climax in the cross and resurrection of Jesus Christ. I am convinced that it is in worship that the self comes closest to truly knowing itself.

The Worshiping Self

I try to make the case for understanding the human self in a relational manner, as one whose identity comes through a lifelong process of addressing and being addressed. I especially understand this "worshiping self" as being one who was created to worship its Creator and finds its true life in doing so. In worship the self finds its place within a community. It finds as well its story, which places its life within a coherent narrative that connects its story with the story of God and God's world. I have employed the basic contours of the Christian story to provide a narrative in which to look at facets of the self's life: creation, fall, salvation, covenant, and consummation. Those facets that roughly correspond to the narrative are: the created self, the sinning and forsaken self, the forgiven self, the ecclesial self, and the eschatological self. I see such a narrative approach to be true to the dynamic nature of God, where the persons of the Trinity are in continuous communication in the mutual indwelling of *perichoresis.* This keeps in balance both the indivisibility of the one God and the distinct identities of the three divine Persons. By analogy, the self is not the product of a private internal process, such as thought or reflection; rather it is a way of being and relating as a personal "I" called out as a dialogue partner, open to others and to God.

It is apparent from the way I treat the various facets of the self in light of the Christian story that I consider the cross and resurrection of Jesus Christ to be the climax and center of the story, from which the entire story derives its meaning. This Christological center correlates with my understanding of the worshiping self, which is "in Christ" — that is, defined both in relationship to other people in community and by one's relationship with God in response to God's grace. This guards against a too-individualistic view of the human self on the one hand, and a too-limited temporal frame on the other.

In examining the self through the various facets of the Christian story, with the help of Isaac Watts's hymns, I have been arguing for a complex and nuanced view of the self. I would call this a "thick" view, which avoids the reductionism that would know the self solely by its pieces and parts, its biological makeup, or its social location, or view it as a static entity or substance. With McFadyen, I see the self as dynamic and lacking an intrinsic center of foundation. The self is dialogical, always in communication with others, and dialectical, never coming to rest, if for no other reason than one never stops being addressed.

I have called this understanding of the self "the worshiping self" because I am convinced that it is in worship that one best knows oneself as addressed by God and as, in Forsyth's phrase, "an object of grace." The word "worship" means to acknowledge God's worth. In worship the self is made aware of its sin, receives the word of forgiveness, is addressed by the Word, and fed by the sacraments. And in the act of singing, the self is joined with the other selves in the congregation, as well as with the great ecumenical church in its width across space and in its breadth across time.

Worship also brings to light the many false gods that invite our attention, and dethrones them as idols before the true God. In worship, too, the self knows its need of others and of God, and keeps its own life from becoming a false center rather than an open process of communication.

Finally, the worshiping self looks beyond its own temporal frame in promise and hope for the day when God will be fully known and rightly worshiped. If the chief end of man is "to enjoy God forever," then the worshiping self finds its true life as part of the great congregation that worships joyfully in heaven. As Watts put it, our destiny is "to sing and love as angels do" (Hymn 42). For now the worshiping self experiences a foretaste of that joy in singing to God in worship:

> Enter his gates with songs of joy,
> With praises to his courts repair
> And make it your divine employ
> To pay your thanks and honours there. (Psalm 100)

15. Spirit and Flesh in Baptism

J. Barry Vaughn

"A three-fold cord, not easily broken" was Anglican theologian Richard Hooker's vivid phrase describing the interrelationship of scripture, tradition, and reason in Christian theology. Scripture speaks with a relatively univocal voice about human nature. Reason (in the form of the sciences) has also come to some fairly firm conclusions. Reason may also take another form — theological reason. There are two primary ways that the tradition speaks: in the voice of the church assembled in council and in the liturgy. This paper will look primarily at how the tradition as embodied in the church's baptismal liturgies speaks to us about human nature.

Baptismal Liturgy

When we turn to the tradition as it is embodied in the church's liturgies, we find that it echoes the witness of Scripture and reason. Indeed, I would argue that baptism is the basic Christian statement about human nature. The goodness of human nature (and all of matter) is displayed by a liturgy, especially by the Christian sacraments, that consistently assume the capacity of flesh and matter to be bearers of divine grace. An exegesis of the church's baptismal liturgies illustrates the point.

If as the authors of *Whatever Happened to the Soul?* believe, the human being is a single unit, not separable into physical and spiritual components, then it would also seem reasonable to assume that the church's rites are also a single unit. In other words, that what we do with our bodies or with water and oil and bread and wine is no less "spiritual" than what is happening when we sit or kneel quietly with our eyes closed (or open). This is exactly what the Fathers teach about the sacraments, especially baptism.

Baptism everywhere assumes the interpenetration and inseparability of the spiritual and the physical. Tertullian articulates the capacity of the physical to be a vessel of the spiritual perhaps more eloquently than any of the other Fathers. He dwells at length on the capacity of the baptismal water to be a vehicle of the Spirit:

> You are bound, my friend, to have in reverence first the antiquity of the waters, that they are an ancient thing, and then the honour done them, that they are the resting place of the Spirit of God, more pleasing to him at that time [i.e., creation] than the other elements . . . only the liquid, a material always perfect, joyous, simple, of its own nature pure, laid down there a worthy carriage for God [to move upon] . . . the liquid was the first to bring forth that which should have life, so that in baptism it need be no wonder if waters already know how to make alive . . . there is no doubt whether God has brought into service in his very own sacraments that same material which he has had at his disposal in all his acts and works, and whether this which is the guide of earthly life makes provision of heavenly things besides.[3]

In commenting on the use of oil, he notes that "the unction flows upon the flesh, but turns to spiritual profit, just as in the baptism itself there is an act that touches the flesh, that we are immersed in water, but a spiritual effect, that we are set free from sins."[4]

Finally, Tertullian explains that God allows the imposition of hands to convey the Holy Spirit to the newly baptized person: "Human ingenuity has been permitted to summon spirit to combine with water, and by application of a man hands over the result of their union to animate it with another spirit of excellent clarity: and shall not God be permitted, in an organ of his own by the use of holy hands, to play a tune of spiritual sublimity?"[5]

Recognizing that the newly baptized may have difficulty seeing beyond the symbolism of baptism to the spiritual realities beyond, John Chrysostom reminds them that they must "develop spiritual eyes . . . so that when you see the font with its water and the hand of the priest touching your head, you will not think that this is mere water nor that it is simply the hand of the bishop that is laid upon your head. It is not a man who performs the rites but the gracious presence of the Spirit who sanctifies the natural properties of the water and who touches your head along with the hand of the priest."[6]

The witness of scripture is that human nature is holistic, not dualistic. While the Gnostics held that the body is at best an irrelevance and at worst an impediment, the Christian faith holds that God is as interested in flesh as in spirit, and this is never more vividly illustrated than in baptism.

Perhaps more than any other Christian rite, baptism is a rite of the entire body. It is a profoundly physical act and has always and everywhere included the use of water. Up through at least the fourth and fifth centuries copious amounts of water were used. E. A. Yarnold states,

> The early accounts of this rite suggest that the candidate stood about waist-deep in water, and was immersed by bowing forward with the bishop's hand pressing on his forehead. . . . However a different impression is given by the fonts belonging to the period that have been discovered and the pictures of the ceremony that have survived, particularly representations of the baptism of Christ which are apparently modeled on the contemporary liturgical practice. In many places it seems that the font was too small for the candidate to immerse his whole body, even if he bent. He must have stood in water that came scarcely above his knees while the minister poured water on to his head.[7]

Regardless, baptism in the early church involved enough water literally to embrace the baptized. Ambrose interprets baptismal immersion as a type of Christ's death and burial: "When you are immersed you receive the likeness of death and burial, you receive the sacrament of his cross; because Christ hung upon the cross and his body was fastened to it by the nails. So you are crucified with him, you are fastened to Christ, you are fastened by the nails of our Lord Jesus Christ lest the devil pull you away. May Christ's nail continue to hold you, for human weakness seeks to pull you away."[8]

Theodore of Mopsuestia borrows the images of a crucible and a potter's wheel to explain the significance of immersion: "So the water you enter is like a crucible in which you are reshaped to a higher nature: you lay aside your old mortality and assume a nature that is completely immortal and incorruptible. You are born in water because you were formed originally from earth and water, and when you fell into sin the sentence of death made you totally corruptible. This is what a potter does when a vase he is shaping from clay becomes spoilt: he shapes it again in water and so it recovers its true form."[9]

Furthermore, baptism in the early church engaged all the senses. It is obvious how baptism engages the sense of feeling and hearing. The spoken words of the liturgy engage the ear, and the water and imposition of the bishop's hands engage the sense of touch.

The pre- and post-baptismal anointings also engaged the sense of smell. Most early liturgies included at least two anointings, an anointing for exorcism prior to baptism and an anointing for the gift of the Spirit following baptism. In commenting on why the baptized is anointed on the nostrils before baptism, Ambrose explains that the bishop "touches the nostrils so that you may receive the sweet fragrance of eternal goodness; so that you can say as the holy apostle said: 'We are the aroma of Christ to God' (2 Corinthians 2:15); and so that the full fragrance of faith and devotion may dwell in you."[10]

Baptism in the early church may also have been a powerful visual experience. Hippolytus mentions that baptism took place "at the hour when the cock crows" after an all-night vigil.[11] The use of candles and lamps in baptism is not well-documented, but as Yarnold points out, "[t]he use of lights must in any event have been necessary in a dawn ceremony." He cites a sermon of Gregory of Nazianzus, who associates the enlightenment received in baptism with the parable of the wise and foolish maidens: "The lamps which you will light symbolize the torchlight procession in the next world, in which our shining, virgin souls will meet the bridegroom with the shining lights of faith."[12] Furthermore, some of the Fathers spoke of baptism as "enlightenment."[13] In any event, the passage from the darkened baptistery into the brightly-lighted church for the newly baptized's first Eucharist must have been visually dramatic.

In an Easter eve sermon, Augustine urged his flock to "[b]e watchful and continue in your watchfulness, for it is this humble and lowly attitude of expectation which turns our night into a shining day. *In this house of prayer we have lit all the lights* [emphasis added]. May God, who once caused light to shine in the darkness by his word, cause light to blaze forth in our hearts, so that we may be inwardly illumined."[14]

Neither did baptism neglect the sense of taste. Hippolytus adds a touch not found in other baptismal liturgies. According to the *Apostolic Tradition* a newly baptized person's first communion included not only bread and wine but also a cup of water and a cup of milk and honey mixed together.[15]

Perhaps the most dramatic way that baptism in the early church was an act of the entire person was by requiring him or her to remove his or her clothes. Catechumens removed their clothes before the pre-baptismal anointing to underscore their complete renunciation of their old lives and their complete acceptance of their new lives in Christ. Cyril of Jerusalem likens the catechumens' nakedness to Christ on the cross and to Adam:

> Stripped naked, in this too you were imitating Christ naked on the cross.
>
> You truly mirrored our first-created parent Adam, who stood naked in paradise and was not ashamed.[16]

However, baptism also recognizes that human nature is also fallen and flawed. Orthodox scholar Alexander Schmemann writes,

> In the baptismal rite, which is an act of liberation and victory, the exorcisms come first because on our path to the baptismal font we unavoidably "hit" the dark and powerful figure that obstructs this path. It must be removed, chased away, if we are to proceed. The moment that the celebrant's hand has touched the head of a child of God and marked it with the sign of Christ, the Devil is there defending that

which he has stolen from God and claims as his possession. We may not see him but the Church knows he is there. We may experience nothing but a nice and warm family "affair," but the Church knows that a mortal fight is about to begin whose ultimate issue is not explanations and theories but eternal life or eternal death.[17]

Lutheran scholar Robert Jenson emphasizes the importance of the exorcism as a part of the baptismal rite:

Modern orders regularly omit exorcism. In the eighteenth century, this is understandable. But that it should still be so, in the late twentieth century, is astonishing: as usual, the church is the last to catch on. The experience of evils that are less than all individual wills, yet manifest all the characters of individual will, i.e., the experience of "the demonic," is *the* experience of our age. If such forces can indeed not be addressed, nor execrated by the gospel, we are all lost in any case.[18]

Exorcism in one form or another seems to have been a part of Christian baptism since at least the middle of the second century. In the *Apostolic Tradition,* Hippolytus writes that the bishop "laying his hand on them [i.e., the baptized] shall exorcize every evil spirit to flee away from them and never to return to them henceforward. And when he has finished exorcizing, let him breathe on their faces and seal their foreheads and ears and noses."[19] In *De Spectaculis,* Tertullian writes that "When we have entered the water, we make profession of the Christian faith in the words of its rule: we bear public testimony that we have renounced the devil, his retinue, and his works." The fourth-century Fathers dwelt at length on the role of exorcism in baptism when they instructed the newly baptized in their catechetical lectures. Cyril of Jerusalem wrote, "You faced westward, heard a voice commanding you to stretch out your hand, and renounced Satan as though to his face."[20]

Baptism cannot be an individual act, because we cannot baptize ourselves. John Chrysostom goes so far as to say that Christ lays his hand on the baptized along with the bishop: "For the priest is not the only one who touches your head; Christ also touches it with his right hand. This is shown by the actual words of the one who baptizes you. He does not say, 'I baptize N.,' but rather, 'N. is baptized.' This shows that he is only the minister of the grace and merely lends his hand since he has been ordained for this by the Spirit. It is the Father, Son and Holy Spirit, the indivisible Trinity, who bring the whole rite to completion."[21] Furthermore, the liturgy of baptism in the early church inevitably culminated in the church's great corporate sacrament of the Eucharist. Chrysostom puts it this way: "As soon as they come up from those sacred waters all present embrace them, greet them, kiss them, congratulate and rejoice with them, because those who before were slaves and prisoners have all at once become free men and sons who are invited to the royal table. For as soon as they come up from the font, they are led to the awesome table which is laden with all good things. They taste the body and blood of the Lord and become the dwelling place of the Spirit; since they have put on Christ, they go about appearing everywhere like angels on earth and shining as brightly as the rays of the sun."[22]

Chrysostom brings us to our final point: baptism does not simply restore the divine image; it is the initial stage of *theosis* or divinization — the journey toward being remade in the image of Christ. In the Byzantine liturgy the prayer over the water beseeches God to "be present . . . in this water and grant that those who are baptized therein may be refashioned, so that they may *put off the old man, which is corrupt according to the deceitful lusts* [Ephesians 4:22], and put on the new man, which is restored after the image of him that created him; that being planted together in the likeness of the death [Romans 6:5] of thy Only-Begotten Son, through baptism, they may share also in his resurrection. . . ."[23] Theodore of Mopsuestia writes, "Then you come up out of the font. . . . You have been born again and have become a completely different person. You no longer belong to Adam, who was subject to change, because he was afflicted and overwhelmed by sin; you belong to Christ, who was entirely free from sin through his resurrection. . . . So it is that he confirms for us the resurrection from the dead and a share in his freedom from corruption."[24]

Conclusion

It is difficult to say which came first: a truncated liturgy of baptism or a truncated doctrine of human nature. However, Robert Jenson puts it well when he writes, "For if baptism says anything at all, it says ending of the old and radically new beginning, right to the physical inconvenience of the bathing; and just this is what Western Christendom has not wanted said. Of course, so long as a ceremony of initiation occurs it says something. What meaningless baptism means is that Christianity demands no renunciation and that grace carries no risks."[25] It does not automatically follow that a liturgy of baptism that more fully follows that pattern of the early church will lead either to more faithful discipleship or a more complete and holistic understanding of human nature created in the divine image, but it is difficult to imagine that if we restore what Yarnold calls the "awe-inspiring rites of initiation" we will not also be in awe of the grandeur of the divine image that God intended us to bear.

16. Rooted: An Anthropology of Preaching

F. Harry Daniel

Oh that I knew how all thy lights combine,
And the configurations of their glorie!
Seeing not only how each verse doth shine,
But all the constellations of the storie.
This verse marks that, and both do make a motion
Unto a third, that ten leaves off doth lie:
Then as dispersed herbs do watch a potion,
These three make up some Christians destinie:
Such are thy secrets, which my life makes good,
And comments on thee: for in ev'rything
Thy words do finde me out, & parallels bring,
And in another make me understood.
Starres are poore books, & oftentimes do misse:
This book of starres lights to eternall blisse.

George Herbert

Seed planting is an image of long-term investment in the future. As such it is a statement of confidence in the future. But at the same time the image engenders a process that is risky and vulnerable, requiring nurture and commitment. The promise and potency of the image are enacted in a context of both tension involving possible failure and powerful, compelling movement toward fulfillment.

"Rootedness" is basic to the fulfillment of the goal of the image, and is the key to resolving the tension between what has already been done and what is yet just promised. Other factors are clearly necessary for full maturation, but rootedness is explicitly basic. Two texts bound together by this image and its vocabulary and which explore the implications of rootedness are the parable of the tares in Matthew 13:24-30 and Ephesians 3:14-21, a parable and a prayer, both of which depend upon hearing and assume that part of what it means to be a human being is to be addressed by an other with a message to be heard. The linkage between these two passages is the verb *rizoomai,* which is rare in the New Testament (Eph. 3:17; Col. 2:7), and its antithetical, but related form *ekrizoō,* found predominately in the gospels (Mt. 13:29; 15:13; Luke 17:6; the only other occurrence is Jude 12). Both Matthew and Ephesians, though in differing contexts, do expand the image through the use of a cultural, architectural metaphor, "grounded" *(themelio):* for Matthew, hearing, meaning to obey Jesus' words, is like being "founded on the rock" (Mt. 7:25); in Ephesians, to be rooted is equivalent to being "grounded," built into love (Eph. 3:17). To be rooted is to share in the innate, inexhaustible God-given human capacity for lifelong growth — yet only when there is no "uprooting," but rather "growing together," and the rootedness is in the overwhelming love of the triune God. How startling! How extravagant!

The heart of Jesus' parable is located in the owner's dialogue with his slaves (13:27-30). The compelling, surprising element is the householder's decision to allow the tares to grow alongside the wheat, and to allow their growth together (*sunauxanō* in the New Testament) until the harvest. Prior to the end time, discipleship is exercised in a *corpus mixtum* in both church and world, which is to be resolved not by human agents at the eschaton, but by angelic ones. Clearly there are "also offensive counterforces and contingently attendant events that are not in accord with the intentions of the reign of God."[26] The world is both a grace-filled and a dangerous place. In the meantime, the mandate is clear: to grow good seed throughout the field of the world.

Strikingly, Matthew's interpretation in 13:36-43 focuses not on the owner's dialogue with his slaves but on the beginning and end of the parable (13:24-26, 30b-d). There is very little hint of the impact of 27-30a and its consequences for human history other than enduring a given, negative situation, which the violent world of the final judgment will resolve. Rather, Matthew's focus is on the time of the uprooting, a theme repeated in 15:13: "Every plant that my heavenly Father has not planted will be uprooted." Matthew's focus is not on the growing together, but on the hope of the separation and the uprooting. This is in line with Matthew's preference for the stark contrasts and reversals of apocalyptic imagery as a means of emphasizing the seriousness of response to and faithfulness in obeying the teaching of Jesus. In fact it is Matthew who adds the full quotation of Isaiah 6:9-10 to confirm the deafness and blindness of the tares.

The Son of Man will do the separating. In the meantime, the allegory both warns against unfaithfulness and encourages patience. Discipleship is to do the will of God now (7:21) so that vindication at the end time will be successful. There will be a separation of life with validity from life that is not valid. Disciples are those who are "founded on the rock." Matthew's counsel is to avoid those attitudes that will bring identification as tares and thus exclusion from the kingdom. A dividing time will come between wheat and tares, sheep and goats, wise and foolish virgins. In the meantime, Christian disciples must endure calculated attempts to destroy their allegiance to the kingdom and their Lord.

The owner's instruction is set in a field-wide context that concerns all. As the rain falls on the just and unjust, as the sun's warmth generates growth in all and thus benefits all life, so the gospel is life-giving and enhancing. At the very least the kingdom of heaven is a process of emergence in the sense that it is always issuing human beings a new challenge to growth.

The presence of the tares provides a forum for risk, novelty, experimentation, and challenge, a relationship that is comfortable with ambiguity and paradox, and yet trusting, responsible, and loving. Such fruitful interference calls forth resistance and arouses a dynamics of new, growing life. Herein lies the extravagance of the parable in its portrait of a gracious owner who encourages co-existence that is challenging, nurturing, and benevolent for kingdom life. It is a common human experience that persons looking in from the outside notice things that those on the inside overlook or do not want to consider, face, or take into account. This may be one level of meaning in the phrase that often concludes Jesus' parables, "Let him who has ears to hear, hear."

To what would tares testify and point? They are attuned to the fragility and suffering of human existence, to the brevity of life and to the conflict between love and death in which death is not defeated. Tares remind and ask wheat, "What does it take to make death fail?" Tares point to the vastness of a universe that is most often deaf to lament and criticize a triumphalism that is insensitive to the power of time to rewrite and destroy life's coherence. Tares are not to be despised, disregarded or destroyed; they are to be heard. They are an invitation to recognize a world of darkness and discontinuity, for it is in that world that faith makes a compelling difference. Christians are rooted and grounded with tares in a violent and dangerous world that we ignore at our peril and over which we must learn to say, "This is God's world." To redirect a statement of Walter Brueggemann, tares "do not permit us to ignore and deny the darkness, personally or publicly, for that is where new life is given, whether on the third day or by some other uncontrolled schedule at work among us."[27] The present world for all its strange mixture of the good and the bad is the kingdom of the Son of Man. And it is that same Son of Man who at the end of time will instruct his angels about the tares. Matthew's phrase "the end of the age" occurs in his interpretation of the parable at 13:39-40, and again at 28:20: "and lo, I am with you until the end of the age." That presence certainly maintains the possibility of dialogue with tares.

The paradox of the parable deepens, for it is the servants of the owner who want to uproot, not the owner, who is wiser and knows that such action would jeopardize all the plants. The will of the owner is that they "grow together." And while the action of the enemy is harmful, it winds up being of benefit to the owner of the harvest of the kingdom.

That such a word of grace is possible in the *corpus mixtum* that is the church (and the world) would require asking in what it is rooted, and inquiring about the character of the Owner. That leads us to Ephesians 3, where both are extravagantly answered.

Ephesians 3:14-21 is a series of doctrinal and hortatory statements cast in the form of a prayer. In 1:17-23 the author had prayed for the enlightenment of all readers. Now at the end of the first major section of the epistle and before the paranetic section he returns to that theme, and in very intense, dense, extraordinary language describes what such enlightenment would look like: it is rooted and grounded in the love of the triune God, consisting of the work of the Father (3:15, 16, 20, 21), Christ

(3:17, 19, 21) and the Spirit (3:16). The prayer is not about potential power available for the accomplishment of its goal, but about God's power to do, to achieve God's goal. This is not human work, but the triune God's work. This is not about what could be; it is about what is.

The goal is to comprehend God's grand design, which is beyond knowledge (3:19), beyond what we can ask or imagine (3:20), and manifested in the love of Christ, leading to being filled with the fullness of God. The gospel's goal is for human beings to progress to a deep understanding of God: to comprehend in verse 18 means to grasp mentally, and to know in verse 19 is a practical grasping or being grasped that comes through personal experience. But even so, the vastness of that which is to be comprehended and known exceeds our control and remains forever inscrutable. To be rooted in such awesome love of the triune God is to experience what it means to be human, and to live and die in the vast dimensions of that love, totally dependent upon it.

The author of Ephesians uses a rich set of terms to describe God's work: the faithful Father whose universal and faithful love blesses all familial-imaged relationships (not simply of blood) and whose direction, care and dominion over creation are exerted in love; the invigorating, empowering, totally committed Spirit who nurtures and transforms inwardly human personality, the life of the soul; and the indwelling Christ who inhabits the heart — the locus of human identity, vitality, intelligence, will, and decision. This is humanity by partnership with the triune God, the God who fills, the Christ who inhabits, and the Spirit who enables and strengthens. To be rooted in this love defined by the triune relationships within God will work its way both within the outsider and within the insider. This is the extravagant secret made known in the gospel. The superabundance of the gospel is dedicated to the faith, hope, love, growth, comprehension, and knowledge of each human being. That it can do this exceeds what we know to ask for or even imagine to be possible. The creative, powerful love of God "calls into existence the things that do not exist" (Rom. 4:17).

To be human is to recognize our lives as gift. We do not exist and then God gifts us; our very existence is gift, and it is God's story of triune love that continues to work passionately and extravagantly in us. That is what rooted means. Our lives become meaningful when we discover and embrace the fact that we are characters in a story we do not create.

What would preaching look like "rooted" in the anthropological world of these two texts? What would make for good preaching? Drawing on the texts discussed above, but also going beyond them, what kinds of generalizations might be made about the role and significance of preaching?

1. Preaching is a matter of passion, perseverance, and pain: passion about the truth in the text that marshals energy, perseverance in pursuing truth so that what is grasped may be thoroughly understood and shared, pain in recognizing the claims of truth and in identifying with and experiencing the agony of the human situation.
2. Preaching is both an art and a craft. As an art, it requires disciplined imagination and creativity; appeal is made to latent, implicit powers. As a craft, it requires attention to method, structure, and medium to develop skills; the focus is on explicit techniques and careful preparation.
3. Preaching is both a de-stabilizing activity and a re-stabilizing activity: in the de-stabilizing of a world dominated by sin and evil, preaching disrupts and disorders; in the re-stabilizing of a world graced and loved by the triune God (Father, Son, and Holy Spirit) who creates, redeems, and sanctifies, preaching re-creates and orders.
4. Preaching is an intentionally communal event.
5. Preaching lives by hermeneutical integrity in which three contexts are carefully explored: that of the text, that of the preacher, and that of the community.
6. Preaching is built upon nurturing and caring for the text, utilizing the best literary-critical and historical-critical resources.
7. Preaching has something to say about the triune God, who is not finished with the creation or us. Without a theocentric focus, preaching becomes just more words in the dizzying cacophony of our time.
8. Preaching is a word from the awesome, passionate, caring, purpose-pursuing, future-creating God.
9. Preaching challenges our bondage to cultural ideologies and enslaving "isms."
10. Preaching is biblical and textual. Though the Biblical message is eternal and universal, its form and setting are always historical and temporal and spatial.

The first question to be asked in the Christian faith is not what should be believed, nor what should be thought, but rather who should be trusted. An answer can be given only through a story of trustworthiness about and from the one trusted. Preaching is about the character of God, and depends upon God's ordered self-disclosure in history. That word emerges with true, powerful love only from profound, life-giving encounters with God's own self — encounters not generated by human beings, but only received by them.

How do we know God is all of the above? In the history of God with the children of Israel and in Christ, who continues to be so characteristically active in all creation. Through texts about this God, God's grace has its own sufficient power and voice.

The Christian faith is rooted in concreteness. Its beginning is found not in religious ideas or universal principles, but in a particular history and story mediated through the lives of human beings in texts. The story, while particular, speaks of the ultimate origin and destiny of all things. Preaching is always bound to the story and avoids translating it into a more acceptable, abstract general principle. The story remains God's story: God has a history. In the words of Robert Jensen, "The original point of trinitarian dialectics is to make the relations between the identities . . . and therewith the temporal structures of evangelical history, constitutive in God."[28] The triune God remains a permanent particular.

Good preaching always remains a struggle, a quest, a goal, but when it comes to expression it may even exceed more than we asked or thought and is better done in the company of tares and a gracious God.

CHAPTER VI

Forms of Neighbor Love

Introduction

Pastor-theologians find their holy calling in gratitude to the Creator that we are created as human souls with the finite freedom to relate in communion with God and other neighbors. When challenged to define just who is our neighbor, Jesus told the parable of the Good Samaritan, which then prompted the Lord's searching counter-query, "Which of these three, do you think, was a neighbor to the man who fell into the hands of the robbers?" (Luke 10:36). The questioner thereby became the questioned as he was confronted with the call of being neighborly himself to all persons in reciprocal need of their own commanded love. Surely any theological investigations of the meaning of being created in the image of a holy and loving God must lead to this same conclusion.

Sonja Hagander deals pastorally with the issue of Christian decision-making from the perspective of her ministry to confused and frustrated college students who do not know "what to do with their lives." They are insecure about their calling because they are uncertain about the will of any sovereign Caller. A part of this generation is generically "religious," but this is most frequently expressed in the form of "privatized spirituality," even in community service. Centered on getting a job in a volatile labor market, "bottom-line"-oriented graduates need help to grapple with an assurance of vocation that includes but also transcends their desire for a ready occupation. The author looks to Luther for relating one's vocation to both expressions of the Triune God's twofold rule of humankind as Creator and Redeemer: demanding law (in promoting justice and judging sin) and promising Gospel (in reckoning justification and guiding sanctification). By clarifying the difference between "doing good" and "doing well," Paul calls all baptized Christians (not just the ordained clergy) "to remain in the condition in which you were called" (1 Cor. 7:20). It is by serving needy neighbors in everyday life that Christians may dedicate their share of the Spirit's vocational gifts to God's glory.

John B. Rogers Jr. provides a wedding sermon on marriage that is based on the church's traditional anthropology as taught in the opening chapters of Genesis, and later cited by Christ in the New Testament parallels of Matthew 19 and Mark 10. The preacher affirms that "something essential and definitive about the human family, and each member thereof, has been decided, declared, and disclosed in Jesus Christ — something we cannot cancel or undo." A God-centered sermon covers such critical issues as (1) God's co-creation of complementary humanity as male and female together in the "image of God"; (2) God's intention for male and female to unite together as "one flesh" in marriage and family within the created order; and (3) God's will that their mutual love be marked by both partners in covenantal fidelity that is both permanent and contributing to the common good.

Confirming this Genesis testimony, Jesus reiterates "the standard, the norm for human community and human sexual expression that reflect the divine intention, and that both Genesis and Jesus see as a gift from the hand of a loving Creator to complete the lives of his human children." Compassion and understanding are advised for those cases that do not conform to or remain within the biblical norm/standard, but the church is declared "not free to ignore or to redefine the biblical standard for marriage in such a way that human preference or cultural pressure usurps the divine purpose."

John Rollefson disagrees. He raises the current controversial issue of same-sex relationships as demanding the church's critical revaluation in light of recent anthropological research in both the scriptures and the sciences. This pastor-theologian speaks with "the ecclesial authority of experience," from the perspective of "scripture, interpreted through the lens of our week-in-and-week-out shared experience as a Christian community, that continues to shape our theological anthropology by keeping us in Spirited conversation with God's living Word." Varied hermeneutical insights are cited from biblical and systematic theologians Choon-Leong Seow, Patrick Miller, Robert Jenson, Paul Jersild, Paul Lehmann, Martha Stortz, and Richard Hays. The church's academic teachers are generally as divided as are members of local congregations on whether gay and lesbian persons should be encouraged or even allowed to join churches, become ordained clergy persons, or be joined in same-sex weddings/unions in church services or civil ceremonies.

While no alternative systematic or exegetical explications are offered here, the author makes clear his own personal view that vague theological inferences and culturally-conditioned practices are not enough to deny the contemporary sanctioning of such publicly committed relationships in church and society. Rather, the divine declaration "It is not good that the man (human one) should be alone" (Gen. 2:18) should clearly override in significance the ancient Genesis etiologies and collectively shared stories of God's original and foundational but not limiting intent in biblical anthropology.

Robert Rice wishes to avoid partisan polemics in his suggestion that the homosexual question before the Christian community is not what constitutes human beings or how we are predisposed genetically or sociologically, but "how God intends for humans to behave." What does it mean to live humanly? The church must arrive at a consensus on a biblical approach to it. While a half dozen or so texts condemn same-sex intercourse, these same texts only elicit another set of reasons for affirming or rejecting them as normative for the whole range of homosexual concerns we face today.

Therefore the author moves on to the foundational level in Christ's teachings on the twofold command to love God and neighbor, "on which hang all the law and the prophets" (Matt. 22:40). That also includes Genesis, of course, and this is how to live humanly. Significantly, the term "righteousness" is used over six hundred times in the Bible to qualify the humans whose relationships are so rightly ordered. "Holiness" and "justice" then serve as connecting bridges for one's righteousness to permeate the requirements and expectations of the dual relationships to God and neighbors.

William Countryman analyzes the Bible's teachings on sex in the corollary terms of purity and property. The New Testament sharpens the Old in its theological judgment that idolatry is the human's root sin, and that all other human practices are to be evaluated in terms of that primal norm. Therefore, the divided Christian community today must think and act humanly in dealing righteously with homosexual persons and life styles.

17. *"What Am I Going to Do with My Life?"*

Sonja Hagander

Often, students will come to me during the academic year, like the young women in Sandburg's poem, "with a peach bloom of young years on them and a laughter of red lips,"[1] wondering what they should do with their lives. Questions come at me, such as, "How do I know I'm in the right major?" "How do I know what God is calling me to do?" "How do I learn how to listen to God's voice?" "Will I have enough money in my job to do what I really want to do in life?" "My dad will be angry with me if I change my major — he wants me to go into business and make a lot of money. How do I tell him what I really want?" All of these questions, of course, are questions of vocation.

Sometimes these questions are smothered in societal trends. Americans often work 60 to 80 hours per week. How many of us look forward to Fridays and fear Mondays? Many work in order to retire. Many work in order to collapse while "on vacation." Some people try to reject this model, only to work in order to have "free time" to do community service or tithe in a "bigger way" on Sundays. And others really do value daily work. They live to work and work to live. So, who are these sons and daughters of these overworked Americans?

The Campus Setting

Who are these college students, and why do our answers to vocation/calling questions need to be framed in light of their questions? It is important to take a moment and look closely at the college setting. It is vital, of course, to understand who is doing the calling; but it is just as important to understand the one who is being called. To state the obvious, we no longer live in Luther's time. Massive modes of learning, being, and teaching have taken place. Students now are not simply deciding between staying in their hometown or moving to a monastery. College students, on the one hand, do not differ so much from the rest of society. But on the other hand, there are some important developmental and cultural aspects to highlight.

Sharon Daloz Parks sets the young adult's faith and meaning-making in the context of The Dream. In a way, she substitutes "dream" for the word "vocation" as she writes,

> Note that the Dream understood through the eyes of the great traditions of faith across time is more than imagining a job or career or profession, narrowly understood. The Dream in its fullest and most spiritual sense is a sense of vocation. *Vocation* conveys "calling" and meaningful purpose. It is a relational sensibility in which I recognize that what I do with my time, talents, and treasure is most meaningfully conceived not as a matter of mere personal passion and preference, but in relationship to the whole of life. Vocation arises from a deepening understanding of both self and world, which gives rise to moments of power when self and purpose become aligned with eternity.[2]

For Parks, like Luther, the concept of relationship must be central to vocation. And for Parks, relationship has everything to do with dependence.[3] Dependence, then, becomes a way of watching the development of faith. There are several forms of dependence that develop as we grow. The movement develops like this:

- Adolescent (dependent/counter-dependent)
- Young Adult (fragile/inner-dependence)
- Tested Adult (confident/inner-dependence)
- Mature Adult (inter-dependence)

Parks is clear about the Young Adult (the "college student") when she writes, "The feelings to which the inner-dependent young adult is therefore correspondingly vulnerable are special forms of bewilderment, loss, and being at sea."[4] For this age group, there is deep ambiguity about growing up. For instance, one young college woman said to me recently as I was encouraging her to think about her gifts to share as an outdoor ministry camp counselor: "I can do whatever I want; I don't want to have any commitment for the summer. . . . My parents support me in whatever I do." The fragile young adult is encouraged into confidence by mentoring; or, in other words, a "word from the outside." I would say this is a point where Luther can help. One of the gifts that Luther brings to this conversation is the impetus of the Living Word coming to us from the outside. Parks echoes this as she writes, "the more tested adult has a deepened capacity to order his or her own sense of value and promise and has become strong enough to let the mentor be other — even to have feet of clay."[5] The Word comes to us calling us as both saint and sinner. Sometimes we accept the Word, and at other times we deny it.

Culturally, today's college students are bombarded with responsibilities. Their generation has been called that of the "organization kid."[6] These young adults "work their laptops to the bone, rarely question authority, and happily accept their positions at the top of the heap as part of the natural order of life."[7] How do we address vocation with these students when they are professional students for four years? How does conversation play a role when they are "goal-oriented"? An activity, whether it entails studying, hitting the treadmill, a drama group, community service, or one of the student groups they found and join in great numbers, is rarely an end in itself; it is a means for self-improvement, resumé-building, and enrichment.[8] But maybe because this generation of students accepts authority and is generally deferential, adults have a window of opportunity to ask specific and ordered questions on vocation, especially since these students are accustomed to structured, organized activities.

A Christian grounding in vocation may seem more dangerous to this generation of students. As David Brooks has pointed out, "The most sophisticated people in preceding generations were formed by their struggle to break free from something. The most sophisticated people in this one aren't." All the more reason to resurrect vocation. What can a profound sense of vocation say to this?

> If you work hard, behave pleasantly, explore your interests, volunteer your time, obey the codes of political correctness, and take the right pills to balance your brain chemistry, you will be rewarded with a wonderful ascent in the social hierarchy.[9]

One strong connection to a discussion of vocation is that a chunk of this generation is "religious." However, according to Brooks, it's a service-oriented, but privatized spirituality:

> I hadn't been on campus more than five minutes before I started hearing about all the students who do community service — tutoring at a

charter school in Trenton, working at Habitat for Humanity–style building projects, serving food at soup kitchens. But religion tends to be more private than public with them, and the character of their faith tends to be unrelievedly upbeat.[10]

A lively discussion of vocation reflecting various Christian voices may lead students to a more public sense of their calling. Augsburg College includes a declaration on vocation in its vision statement:

> Augsburg stresses Luther's understanding that we do not find and live out our callings (exercise our vocations) in order to please God. Instead, vocation is for this life, and is on behalf of this world — for our neighbors.[11]

Luther on Vocation

Many people, even at the Lutheran college where I am situated, believe that vocation relates solely to one's occupation. But looking back 400 years helps to center the conversation regarding vocation. The view stated above is correct in part; it shows at least a hunch that one's calling does have to do with life in this world. Along with this, viewing vocation purely as service to one's neighbor leaves out a God who is active in an ongoing way in creation. This reminds us that it is vital not to let vocation fall to the lowest common denominator of service. Often in conversations regarding vocation, the creative aspect permeates, and the redemptive aspects are sequestered or totally lost. Just take a peek at some current titles on vocation: "Whistle While You Work," and "Callings: Finding and Following an Authentic Life."

It is necessary to be reminded of Luther's view of the law in order to discuss vocation. There are two uses of the law — the first and the second use. The first use of the law clearly is political or civil. It tells me that I will pay a fine for speeding, that I will go to jail for stealing. The second use of the law is theological. Its shows us our sin, convicts us, puts us to death so that the gospel can do its work.[12] The Christian hears the gospel proclaimed and faith is created. Here Luther's view of humans being both saints and sinners is helpful *(simul iustus et peccator)*. Christians still use the law, for Christians cannot keep it willingly in any special way. Christians are to be "put to death and raised to new life" again and again. This leads to what cannot be left out of Luther.

The gospel brings this new life again and again. From faith, good works flow. Luther does not let the Christian focus only on "heaven." We are freed to focus our daily lives on our neighbor.[13] Central to Luther's view on vocation is Christ. God's coming into the world to redeem it shows forth God's ongoing commitment to creative work in the world. Vocation is an incarnational theology. Vocation relates to all aspects of life. This is so clearly stated by Luther:

> How is it possible that you are not called? You have always been in some state or station; you have always been a husband or wife, or boy or girl, or servant. Picture before you the humblest estate. Are you a husband, and you think you have not enough to do in that sphere to govern your wife, children, domestics, and property so that all may be obedient to God and you do no one harm? Yea, if you had five heads and ten hands, even then you would be too weak for your task, so that you would never dare to think of making a pilgrimage or doing any kind of saintly work.[14]

Luther makes it clear that vocation is the calling that refers to all relationships and situations, not only one's occupation. He also emphasizes that when it comes to work, he is not talking about religious work per se. All places are situations in which to work out one's calling. For instance, my vocation involves being a wife, daughter, sister, pastor, coworker, community member, public citizen, musician, and more. Romans 12 and 1 Corinthians 12 speak clearly about the holistic calling of humans in society. Luther includes these scripture passages in his writings on vocation:

> It is to be lamented that no man is content and satisfied with that which God gives him in his vocation and calling. Other men's conditions please us more than our own. . . . The more we have, the more we want. To serve God is for every one to remain in his vocation and calling, be it ever so mean and simple.[15]

Harold H. Ditmanson, faculty emeritus at St. Olaf, echoed Luther when he wrote,

> The Christian faith has a universal relevance to every aspect of human life. It is interested in science, history, literature, psychology, art, and politics. It has something to say about all of them, though it does not claim a technical authority within these spheres. It is concerned with every aspect of human relationship, personal and public. It is concerned above all with the interior life of each individual, the deepest level of one's being.[16]

Luther's concept of vocation draws strength from the fact that for Luther, as for Ditmanson, all of life is seen in relationship to God. To push this to the extreme in terms of vocation would mean that vocation is understood only in terms of natural law.[17] This carries with it two slippery slopes. On one slope, we slide into the status quo, which appears to be divinely blessed, or we slide into chaos that is viewed as "against God." On the other slope, we slide into individualism. The societal relationship is lost and our actions have only individual moral value. These two very slippery slopes are mountains that must be climbed in the dialog with twenty-first-century writings on calling or vocation.

Some interpreters of Luther have feared that this is where Luther leaves us — on the slippery slope of either status quo/chaos or individualism. However, Gustaf Wingren challenges this mode of thinking and refreshingly brings us back to vocation in light of creation and redemption. Each of us is both saint and sinner. Wingren writes:

> Since man is at the same time both old and new, so both works of God, the law and the gospel, proceed at the same time. In the activity of daily living, it is impossible to distinguish what are respectively the actions of the old man and of the new. Unwillingness and joy, antagonism and love are so intertwined that God alone sees which is which. . . . Man's outward life is filled with demands, and the many responsibilities are frightening. But at the same time faith lifts him up in freedom above neighbor and vocation; and in this very freedom from law he finds joy in stooping down to serve his neighbor. The Christian knows both joy and fear at the same time.[18]

Reviving Luther's concept of vocation is dangerous. It forces us to see ourselves once again in relationship to the people, the institutions, the God among us. To read only current bestsellers on vocation is to face the temptation to cling to a self-serving concept of vocation, which may be related only to one's occupation, or solely focused on "finding oneself." By reading Luther we cannot miss that we are all called. Often a college student will ask a question like, "How do I know I'm doing what God wants me to do?" To set the answer in light of Luther on vocation is helpful. Luther reminds us that not even a sparrow "falls to the ground without the will of our heavenly Father, and that all the hairs of our head are numbered."[19] Our relationship with God and God's relationship with us is vital in the conversation on vocation.

Only vocation based on Luther's thought is capable of answering and guiding the questions of today's college student — and, for that matter, all of us. This world is full of competing powers and struggles that are apparent each day. Vocation is for this world and is quite situational. Vocation is done for this world and is focused on the neighbor. H. Richard Niebuhr clarifies this stance:

> Luther's answer to the Christ-and-culture question was that of a dynamic, dialectical thinker. Its reproductions by many who called themselves his followers were static and undialectical. They substituted two parallel moralities for his closely related ethics. As faith became a matter of belief rather than a fundamental, trustful orientation of the person in every moment toward God, so the freedom of the Christian [person] became autonomy in all the spheres of culture. It is a great error to confuse this parallelistic dualism of separated spiritual and temporal life with the interactionism of Luther's gospel of faith in Christ working by love in the world of culture.[20]

Niebuhr hints at a model of vocation that emphasizes *primary calling* and *secondary calling.* This is drawn from the word *vocare* itself, meaning to call out. One cannot be called without a Caller. Our primary calling comes from God, the Caller, and our secondary callings come from our relationships with one another and with ourselves, our work, our responsibilities, our life experiences. There is constant ebb and flow within this primary call and secondary call.

18. "Whom God Hath Joined Together"

John B. Rogers Jr.

What understanding of the nature of the human self do we take with us into the pastoral tasks of preaching, teaching, the "cure of souls," and Christian witness and service in the common life? What have we learned, and what have we still to learn, from scripture and from the history of Christian thought and piety about what it means to be human? What might we learn from and contribute to conversations about anthropology with the natural and human sciences, as well as with those artists, writers, and musicians who probe the mystery of the human?

The gospel announces that something essential and definitive about the human family, and each member thereof, has been decided, declared, and disclosed in Jesus Christ — something we cannot cancel or undo. For all we may hear and learn from conversations with other disciplines, therefore, we cannot leave our theological/Christological perspective aside. Nor can we simply use our perspective to refine, or as a predicate to, a definition of the human self formulated apart from biblical and Christological considerations.

Human beings are not self-defined; we are God-defined (Christ-defined?), God-claimed, even God-haunted. To go about ministry with some understanding of what it means to be human that ignores God as the giver of our identity or diminishes the sovereignty of God while encouraging the sovereignty of self results in a gospel that at best commends itself as useful, rather than true.

A church that simply mirrors the world in its language will never claim the world for its Lord. A church that defines itself on society's terms, that tries to live by the agenda of the prevailing culture, that allows the world to determine its mission and its message is headed toward incomprehensible failure and irrelevance.

Men and women of all sorts and conditions still need witness to the presence of God as the native climate of the human heart in which we know ourselves to be at home. Human beings still grope for meaning: in their homes, in their work, in their unemployment, in hospitals, in nursing homes, in precinct meetings, at the foot of a grave, in the shadow of a cross, in the glory of a sacramental moment. And this calls for pastoral wisdom that can act and speak credibly of meanings that surpass experience, even if with a stammering tongue and fallible action. Human beings deserve to understand their existence as from God, human life lived before God, each and every life claimed, corrected, and redeemed by God, all life for time and eternity belonging to God and upheld in God's encompassing presence and omnipotent grace. Our privilege is to nurture in our people, and in each other, a deep awareness that life is finite but not happenstance, that all its goods are gifts, that come weal or woe God is for us, and that nothing can separate us from the love of God in Christ Jesus our Lord.

In this vocation, we pastors are, among other things, "stewards of the mysteries of God." Surely one of the "mysteries of God" is the human self/soul that is "hidden with Christ in God" (Col. 3:3). The following sermon was preached during the past year and was occasioned by issues in the life of church and culture to which Christian faith, and the Christian understanding of the human self, have a timely word to speak. "Whom God Hath Joined Together" is a version of a wedding sermon delivered on the occasion of my son's marriage — a sermon that I revised and expanded significantly for my congregation.

Whom God Hath Joined Together (Matt. 19:1-12)

Our New Testament lesson is one of two occasions in the gospels where Jesus' opponents set a theological trap for him with marriage as bait — a rather crafty trick to play on a bachelor. It didn't work either time. The Pharisees regarded marriage as something that will yield to our management and manipulation. Jesus says if you really want to understand marriage, don't talk about a human arrangement. Start with the scriptures, the power of God, and the purpose of God for human existence.

"Is it lawful," the Pharisees had asked, "to divorce one's wife for any cause?" (Matt. 19:3, cf. Mark 10:2) The rabbis have their differences on this matter. . . . What say you, Rabbi Jesus? What is permissible? What are our rights, our possible advantages under the Law? Permission? You know what's permitted, said Jesus in effect. Better that you know God's purpose — indeed, God's command. And then, in both Matthew's and Mark's account, Jesus quotes from Genesis. From the beginning of creation,

> God made them male and female. For this reason a man shall leave his father and mother and be joined to his wife, and the two shall become one flesh. So they are no longer two but one. What therefore God has joined together, let no one put asunder. (Mark 10:6-9)

Undergirding life itself, and our lives in particular, are God's gracious will, God's intentional love, God's faithful purpose that from the foundation of the world have held and guided us, and that will never let us go. Apart from God's intention in these matters, we cannot hope to get life and relationships right — whatever might be "permitted," or desired.

I.

> From the beginning of creation, "God made them male and female. . . . In the image of God, God created them."

Jesus faces us with God's creation of humanity as male and female so wondrously described in our Old Testament lesson. The story tells of the common origin of man and woman in the will and intention of God. Human existence, say Genesis and Jesus, is co-existence, existence in community and mutuality, intended and given by a gracious and loving Creator to complete that which in itself is not yet complete.

In our Old Testament lesson (Gen. 1:26-28a, 31; 2:4b-5a, 7-8, 18-25), we start to read,

> Then the Lord God said, "It is not good that the man should be alone. . . ."

Where God looks upon all creation, as he does in the hymn-like account of creation in Genesis 1, and pronounces it "Good . . . very good," if something is "not good" we are to understand that it is not done, not complete. Apart from one with whom Adam can co-exist, co-respond, human existence is incomplete.

And so God forms the beasts — the creatures of earth and air. Adam names the creatures, and they serve him. Human sovereignty, however, only points to what is still lacking, to what Adam cannot secure for himself, to what only God can provide for, to what he can only be given, as he was given his own life, to what he can only receive as a gift, even as he in turn is himself made a gift.

> So the Lord caused a deep sleep to fall upon the man, and while he slept God took one of his ribs. . . . And the rib which the Lord God had taken from the man he made into a woman and brought her to the man.

This sleep effectively removes the man from any participation, or possible claim of such, in the creation of woman. Adam thus has no "rights" to assert, no claims to make regarding this other. The creation of the woman is a divine action. The man does not participate except as one upon whom God acts.

> In the image of God . . . male and female, God created them.

Adam is not even granted the prerogative of discovering this other one. He does not search her out and take her to himself. God brings her to Adam as the original "father of the bride." Here is neither dominance nor submission, only gratitude that erupts in joy:

> Ah! At last! Bone of my bones, and flesh of my flesh.

The wonder and mystery of the woman and of her origin in God are obvious to the man. He is no longer alone. The man and the woman are in relationship — co-existing, co-responding, completing each other, gifts to each other. And that, at last, is good.

II.

Good, yes, but perhaps one should not so quickly say, "At last." Neither this first human relationship, nor any human relationship, even one as wondrous as marriage, is an end in itself, either in fact or in this powerful story. Adam seems to have thought so: "This *at last* is bone of my bones . . . !" But anyone who has ever been in love will understand his getting carried away.

The story goes on to ground marriage and family in the created order as part of the divine intention. The physical union of man and woman, wondrous and without shame, the birth of children, the creation of a home — these are not incidental, but are foundational to human existence. Because

> From the beginning of creation God made them male and female. . . . Therefore a man leaves his father and mother and cleaves to his wife, and they become one flesh. (Genesis 2:24)

The expression "one flesh" refers primarily to the physical union of husband and wife in sexual intimacy. And yet, the one life (one flesh!) that comes of this union in the birth of a child cannot be ignored. Human birth is not the mere incidental byproduct of sexual intimacy, but is built into the structure of creation by divine intention.

Even so, we cannot say, "At last," for more wondrous still, and more profound, is that in being made thus to co-respond, humanity is made ready for God. Whatever the story tells us about marriage, about family, about intimacy — and it tells us a great deal about these things — it is even more profoundly a story about human beings made ready, prepared from the foundation of the world for the grace of God. Just a few short verses later, when God comes looking for Adam and Eve, God engages them personally. God speaks to them as "I" to "thou." In the correspondence fundamental to our human nature and being, we catch sight of God's eternal intention to come to us as God, and to be with us and for us personally.

And then, "in the fullness of time," as we shall be reminded often over the coming season of Advent, the word of God sounded again in the ear of a young woman of Nazareth. "Let there be . . . Emmanuel — God with us . . . and it was so." The Word became flesh and dwelt among us, full of grace and truth, claiming our lives and relationships for God, and drawing us into the very life of God. So that the author of Hebrews, in a compelling commentary on our Genesis lesson, wrote,

> For (Christ) who makes holy and those who are made holy have all one origin. That is why he is not ashamed to call them brothers and sisters, saying. . . . "Here am I, and the children God has given me." (Hebrews 2:11, 13)

III.

Now we can say, "At last." We are a long way from where the Pharisees began with Jesus. Jesus, however, had a reason for taking them, and us, into the deeps of life and love as God intends them. Jesus knew that to take God's gift of marriage and reduce it to a legal structure was to invite precisely that attitude that is always asking after rights and advantages, loopholes and edges. From there it is not very far to the pain and chaos of marriage commitments casually regarded and easily abandoned.

Jesus did know that marriage is sustained by wonder at the mystery of the other; and without this wonder, a relationship almost inevitably degenerates into exploitation. Jesus did know that marriage is nurtured by reverence for the intimacy, the knowledge, the unity whereby a man and woman are bound to one another in mutual obligation, responsibility, and permanence. Jesus did know that to hear the story of Genesis in the midst of our own particular situation, with whatever pain, confusion, and brokenness that may include, is to be reminded of another Life — that Life, as one hymn puts it, "by which alone we live" — the One by whom and for whom we are made, to whom we belong and must give account, and apart from whom we are restless and vulnerable in our lives and relationships to all sorts of heartache.

Whom therefore God has joined together, let no one put asunder.

IV.

So right, so neat, so ideal that all sounds. And then we look at this imperfect, broken, painfully real world where all of us live and love, never as fully as we ought to and want to, this world where the church has its ministry of pastoral care and justice and compassion, this world where our performance within God's purpose often leaves both us and God heartbroken. And we ask, haltingly perhaps, and with some real sadness: Does this mean that all marriages, by definition, express God's will? No. Marriage, like any gift of God, can be and too often is damaged by infidelity, broken by abuse, destroyed by neglect. No. Marriage is not immune to the destructive power of human sin and selfishness. Because marriage is God's gift to his human creatures, therefore a particular marriage may express God's will more or less faithfully. But a particular marriage also may express God's will not at all.

Does this mean that divorce is wrong? Sometimes it is, yes. Sometimes it is not. Always divorce takes its toll on a human heart and spirit, even when divorce is absolutely necessary to end a marriage that is terribly wrong and is exacting its own toll. There is always a tragic aspect to divorce. Promises made have not been kept. Vows to love, honor, cherish have been broken, and now a home and hearts are so broken that if life is to go on under any semblance of physical, emotional, and mental health, a marriage must be ended. Some, Jesus said, do not, will not, cannot live into or up to the demands of this gift. And those women and men and children wounded and scarred by the pain of divorce need the church's love and support, not its scorn or neglect. I have had more than a few members of my congregation say what we as a church family have meant to them in the throes and aftermath of a marriage that has ended.

Yes, and there are also those whom, God forgive us, we have failed. So much of the church's ministry of nurture and pastoral care seeks to strengthen lives of individuals and families against the forces that pull people apart and cause lives and relationships to come undone. But we must stay with people, and not pull back, when lives and hearts are broken. In all such situations, surely "the love of Christ constrains us" (2 Cor. 5:14).

Does this mean that only those who marry conform to the will of God? No. Listen again to Eugene Peterson's rendering of the Matthew passage:

> But Jesus said, "Not everyone is mature enough to live a married life. It requires a certain aptitude and grace. Marriage isn't for everyone. Some, from birth seemingly, never give marriage a thought. Others never get asked — or accepted. And some decide not to get married for kingdom reasons. But if you are capable of growing into the largeness of marriage, do it.

The single life, whether by choice or by circumstance, has its own disciplines, decisions, and demands; its own relationships, rewards, and responsibilities; its own opportunities and obligations. In every stage of my life, and in every church I have served, and in every community in which I have lived, my life and the life of our family have been blessed by the lives of single women and men who, because of their gift for opening their lives to others, and taking others into their lives, can in no sense be said to "live" alone, even though they may dwell alone.

Does this mean that marriage is, or that family relationships are, the only acceptable form of close human relationships? No. The Bible knows and encourages friendship: friendship between members of the opposite sex, friendship between members of the same sex, friendship between people of different ages. And the Bible commends the virtues of trust, faithfulness, and responsibility that accompany such relationships. Jesus' own relationships outside his family were of this very nature — friendships that, from every indication, were dear and precious to him. One thinks of his friendship with Mary and Martha and their brother Lazarus, of his friendship with his disciples. "Love one another," he commanded, "as I have loved you." "I have called you friends," which must have been among the most thrilling things he ever said to them. Without for a moment denying the majesty and mystery of God, those words speak tenderly to us of the *friendship* of God.

Paul's letters to the young churches are filled with expressions of his own affection for sisters and brothers in faith, and with exhortations for them to love one another. And his word was apparently heeded, because the early Christian church was distinguished by the remarkable way in which the people related to each other — even as they held themselves to a higher and stricter standard of sexual behavior and fidelity than the culture of the Greco-Roman world either encouraged or modeled.

So we live with this gift of humanity as male and female, this gift of marriage between man and woman. And we live toward and into and under God's purpose that sustains this gift *in a fallen world.* God's gift suffers from our abuse and failure. We ourselves suffer pain. Frustrated hopes are not realized. Many of our preferred ways of being related reflect the fallenness and brokenness of creation. For example, sexual abuse and infidelity within marriage, casual sex, recreational sex — I think the current jargon is "hooking up" — intimacy without commitment, union of bodies without union of souls. This is what can happen when we prefer to set our own definitions of what it means to be human and seek our own advantages under our own arrangements.

V.

Jesus points to Genesis as the expression from the beginning of God's intention for human existence, of God's general will for sexual life, of God's provision for the propagation of the human race. From the beginning of creation,

> God made them male and female. For this reason a man shall leave his father and be joined to his wife, and the two shall become one flesh. So they are no longer two but one. What therefore God has joined together, let no one put asunder. (Mark 10:6-9)

Here is the standard, the norm for human community and human sexual expression that reflect the divine intention, and that both Genesis and Jesus see as a gift from the hand of a loving Creator to complete the lives of his human children. This is why the marriage service in our *Book of Common Worship* declares,

> God has established and sanctified marriage for the welfare and happiness of his people. Our Savior has declared that a man shall leave his father and mother and be joined to his wife. By his apostles he has instructed those who enter into this relation to cherish a mutual esteem and love; to bear with each other's infirmities and weaknesses; to comfort each other in sickness, trouble, and sorrow . . . to provide for each other . . . to pray for and encourage each other . . . and to live together as the heirs of the grace of life.

As for cases that do not conform to or remain within the biblical standard? Persons in these various relationships are children of God for whom the church must care with understanding and compassion. In any human relationship, the church in its pastoral ministry must support and encourage the virtues of trust, faithfulness, responsibility, and commitment. Even so, the church is not free to ignore or to redefine the biblical standard for marriage in such a way that human preference or cultural pressure usurps the divine purpose.

VI.

Whom therefore God has joined together let no one put asunder.

As we are not complete without God, so we are not complete without each other. As T. S. Eliot put it in "Choruses from the Rock,"

> What life have you if you have not life together?
> There is no life that is not in community
> And no community not lived in praise of God.

But just because God made us for each other, and just because God claims and provides for us as his own precious children, so we can claim the gift of each other in God's gift of marriage — and despite fallenness and failure, live together as heirs of the grace of life.

Amen.

19. *The Church and Same-Sex Relationships*

John Rollefson

"Sexual issues are tearing our churches apart today as never before," writes Walter Wink in an article titled "Homosexuality and the Bible." He continues,

> The issue of homosexuality threatens to fracture whole denominations, as the issue of slavery did a hundred and fifty years ago. We naturally turn to the Bible for guidance and find ourselves mired in interpretive quicksand. Is the Bible able to speak to our confusion on this issue?[21]

My experience as a pastor who has served three quite different congregations over the last quarter century and my present university congregation for more than a decade leads me to answer Wink's troubling question with a resounding "Yes!" Yes, the Bible has spoken and continues to speak to us who gather week in and week out in church to hear God's Word and share the Supper. Moreover, the Bible speaks in a way that has helped us as faith communities to hear a clarifying and unifying Word that is good news amid the larger church's "confusion on this issue."

This is due, in large part, to the "hermeneutical ecology" that is created by the presence in our midst of fellow Christians who happen to be gay and lesbian. Their embodied experience of same-sex relationships, from friendships to committed partnerships, is a part of our common life in the same way as are our heterosexual relationships, from marriages to divorces, single friendships to dating and engaged couples. "Homosexuality" is not an issue that divides us, but is one way of describing an aspect of the personhood of some of those among us that differentiates us and enriches our sense of diversity within the body of Christ. The presence of gay and lesbian fellow believers helps to sharpen the acuity of our listening for God's Word as we hear Jesus' imperative, "Whoever has ears to hear. . . ." Rather than being "mired in interpretive quicksand" over "this issue" in which so much of the church feels "stuck," our community witnesses to the Truth that has set us free, a liberating Word that challenges all forms of enslavement to the powers that be. It is scripture, interpreted through the lens of our week-in-and-week-out shared experience as a Christian community, that continues to shape our theological anthropology by keeping us in Spirited conversation with God's living Word.

> See the work of God;
> for who can make straight what God has made crooked? (Ecclesiastes 7:13)

Choon-Leong Seow, Professor of Old Testament at Princeton Theological Seminary and editor of a collection of essays written by PTS faculty titled *Homosexuality and Christian Community,* cites this text in support of his contention that "creation is not as orderly as one would like to believe." Particularly the wisdom tradition, he contends, while recognizing that God is the Creator of the universe, "also concedes that God's creation does include many irregularities and unevenness — anomalies that no human being can explain or change":

> Wisdom's perspective is admittedly heterodox when judged by the viewpoints of the Torah and the Prophets. The entire corpus of wis-

> dom books defies any attempt to systematize the Old Testament in terms of a definite center. There is not one perspective in the Bible, but many.

Further, Seow argues, the wisdom tradition is a "theology from below (starting with the plight of humanity)" and thereby provides a "necessary counterpoint to the dominant 'theology from above,'" which is often accompanied by a "thus saith the Lord." This means that

> Wisdom literature is thus a persistent reminder to us that we should not be too sure that we speak for God and too slow to admit that we stand with the rest of humanity before the mysteries of God and in the face of life's contradictions.[22]

This leads to the clear implication for Seow that in "wisdom literature we are instructed not to ignore nature, science, reason and experience." Quite the opposite: the biblical wisdom tradition, Seow claims, is itself "*scriptural authority* for human beings to make ethical decisions by paying attention to science and human experiences." "We must not say," he insists,

> as we often hear in the debate about homosexuality, that "experience has nothing to do with it" or that "only scripture matters." It is scriptural to take human observations and experiences seriously.[23]

Patrick Miller, an Old Testament scholar and Seow's colleague at Princeton Theological Seminary, concurs and broadens his remarks beyond the perspective of the Hebrew wisdom tradition within scripture when he observes that "the way of human discernment and reason's sensibility in the light of the complexities we encounter is not something foreign to scripture or disdained by scripture in favor of a simple reading of texts":

> It is scripture itself that teaches us the importance of new knowledge, of the investigation of science, of the proven wisdom that comes from experience and is a part of our fear of the Lord. We tend to set the revelation of scripture condemning homosexual acts against our human desire to be open to the homosexual person and against our sense from

> experience that homosexuality is not finally reducible to the category of sin.

"But that tendency to trump experience with revelation," Miller concludes, "comes up against scripture's own valuing of the wisdom of experience and its insistence that those who fear the Lord are to take account of what knowledge and wisdom teach us."[24]

A particularly egregious example of a theologian's refusal to allow a significant role for science or human experience in the matter under discussion is found in Robert Jenson's breezy pronouncements that "homoeroticism is of course not a mode of sexuality at all, but an escape from it" and "talk of 'same-sex marriage' is a mere triumph of Humpty Dumpty." These summary dismissals of the concerns and shared experience of gay and lesbian Christians stem from Jenson's breathtaking assertion that "no more in this context than in any other do we discover God's creative intent by examining the empirical situation."[25] Of course, "God's creative intent" is not to be found apart from scripture, but neither does our hearing of scripture occur apart from our empirical location, knowledge, and life experience. As Christian ethicist Paul Jersild has written,

> Protestant Christianity rightly affirms the primacy of the Bible, compelling its continuing conversation with it. This conversation requires a careful listening to Scripture, but that listening takes place with "ears" — or minds and hearts — that bring to bear the concerns and perspective of the church's own cultural and social world. In this process, the moral issues of the time stimulate new perspectives in understanding what Scripture and tradition have to say in relation to these issues.[26]

In this matter of homosexual relationships, Jersild further believes, "the church is being challenged to recognize that its own experience in the present moment, in which a once alienated people are being restored, is a powerful reality that cannot be denied by laws out of the past that have consigned these people to perpetual judgment." This leads to the conclusion, *contra* Jenson, that "our experience today as Christians in the world gives the shape and form to the questions we ask of Scripture and therefore to the kinds of answers we discern."[27]

Interestingly, Richard Hays, a vigorous advocate for the church's traditional proscription of same-sex relationships, argues in his widely influential *The Moral Vision of the New Testament* that "it is crucial to remember that experience must be treated as a hermeneutical lens for reading the New Testament," and then adds the important qualifier "rather than as an independent, counterbalancing authority."[28] This is the point I insist upon as well: that experience, as well as science and other empirical realities, are not separate sources of authority within the church, but that they contribute to the creation of the "hermeneutical lens," to use Hays's metaphor, through which Scripture is not only read but understood and interpreted.

Alluding to the struggle described in Acts 10 and 11 through which Peter and the early church changed their minds regarding the inclusion of Gentiles previously counted "unclean" on account of scripture, Hays acknowledges that it was "the experience of uncircumcised Gentiles responding in faith to the gospel message [that] led the church back to a new reading of Scripture." But, he insists, "only because the new experience of Gentile converts proved hermeneutically illuminating of Scripture was the church, over time, able to accept the decision to embrace Gentiles within the fellowship of God's people." So too, Hays concludes, must a reading of Scripture amid a church inclusive of gay and lesbian persons be illuminative of God's original intent in Scripture.[29]

> Well, you got your story and I got mine.
> Difference of Opinion.
> I guess everybody's got a story, right?
> (Charles Baxter, *The Feast of Love,* 264)

> It is not good that the human one should be alone. (Genesis 2:18a)

We hear God's story of the creation of the earthling and the divine declaration of "not good" regarding the earthling's aloneness in conversation with our own and others' yet unfinished human stories. A congregation is like a "complex, ongoing, and multifaceted conversation," Thomas Long suggests, invoking John McClure's phrase, that is "talking itself into becoming a Christian community."[30] Martha Stortz explicates this hermeneutical ecology of the faith community further as she explains in "A Table Talk on Lutheran Ethics,"

> There are intersecting circles of Scripture, church tradition, experience, culture, and so forth. The community needs to take seriously the witness of each of these and somehow come to a point where it can say, "It seems right to the Holy Spirit and to us." All these pieces are present and shape one another. I find that people appeal to experience as if it were raw. But experience is always already shaped, for example, by Lutheran and biblical understandings. There's enormous reflexivity between the way I read Scripture and the way Scripture "reads" me.

"This happens," she concludes, "in the context of community."[31]

Paul Lehmann makes an important contribution to this matter from beyond the grave in his final, posthumously published work, in which he reflects on the Genesis creation accounts. As Patrick Miller observes, Lehmann's comments "are indicative of the fact that what *the text says does not yet tell us what it teaches; that happens only when the text is perceived from some angle of vision*" (my emphasis). Miller goes on to comment, "For Lehmann, as it should be for us all, that angle was the gospel, which is, in his now-familiar formulation, what God was and is doing to make and to keep human life human."[32]

Lehmann's "angle" on the Genesis account is worth citing at length, paying special attention to his crucial distinction between a "limiting" and a "foundational" instance.

> [A] divine ordination is not a *limiting* instance, but a *foundational* one. As a *limiting* instance, the divine ordination to sexual otherness and reciprocity is put forward as the normative mode of sexuality, in relation to which variants are excluded as deviants from the heterosexual norm. As a *foundational* instance, the divine ordination to sexual otherness and reciprocity becomes the liberating instance in relation to which divergent possibilities may be pursued and assessed. As a *limiting* instance, heterosexuality necessarily excludes homosexuality from the divine purpose of and for human fulfillment. As a *foundational* instance of otherness in differentiation and commitment, inequality and heterogeneity, reciprocity and fidelity, heterosexuality becomes the liberating occasion and sign of human fulfillment in relation to which homosexuality may also be affirmed. Just as in Scripture and tradition a central and indispensable correlation between monotheism and monogamy has been discerned and affirmed, yet without requiring the in-

> stantaneous and intransigent rejection of concubinage, polyandry or polygamy, or even interracial and/or interfaith marriage as a test case of the obedience of faith, so the foundational and liberating instance of heterosexuality as a parable of human fulfillment does not require an intransigent rejection of homosexuality as a test case of the obedience of faith.[33]

In light of Lehmann's distinction, Genesis 2:18a can be seen to be an example of God's foundational and thereby liberating rather than limiting intent for humanity (negatively stated): it is *not good* for the human one to be alone. This declaration — not procreation, not sexual complementarity, not plumbing (*pace* Jenson!), not the institution of marriage, not the "heterosexual order of creation,"[34] not whatever other etiologies may be found in the second creation account, however important they may be — sounds most loudly and clearly within our congregational hearing and conversation as God's original and foundational but not limiting intent from which all the rest follows. It is this Word of God that makes most sense of our collectively shared stories, and that speaks to us the good and liberating news that relationship — that not being alone — marks the beginning of our being truly human and, in Lehmann's words, is what "keeps us human."

Beginning with our first year together as pastor-theologians, we seem to have arrived at a broad consensus regarding the nature of the Bible as the church's book and its peculiar authority as experienced within the life of the gathered worshiping community. The insights of biblical scholars and theologians working individually and together on various projects have offered us special insights and stimulated our own conversation. But they have not displaced the ecclesial authority we experience within our living, worshiping communities that gather regularly to hear the Word and share the supper and then disperse for the sake of ministry in daily life. Our local congregations are not the whole church but they are fully church as they confess themselves to be participants in the "one, holy, catholic and apostolic church." Our local ecclesial communities are not an ideal and abstract church but are a real and embodied gathering of saints/sinners who know and care for one another and the mission of the Gospel into which they have been baptized. Here God's Word speaks to the lives and within the hearts of its hearers and is heard and bears fruit — or it does not. In this sense the congregation constitutes the primary "hermeneutical ecology" to which this essay has tried to pay attention.

The preceding is far from all that needs to be said about this conflicted matter we call "homosexuality" in the life of the church. It is, I would argue, that area of the church's contemporary life most reflective of a theological anthropology gone awry. A place from which we might begin afresh, I believe, is with Yahweh's original "not good," with the Creator's definitive dissatisfaction not with humanity itself but with the result of the human one's being alone. This as the originating Word of our conversation with scripture regarding the basis for our theological anthropology is one that at the very least calls into question all church rule-making that would seek to isolate people from meaningful, committed and mutually fulfilling human relationship. It is a Word that at least one community of Christians finds to be a liberating and not limiting text that by the inspiration of the Spirit has the power to make and keep making us — but not only us — church.

20. *What It Means to Live Humanly*

Robert S. Rice

During the past quarter century an incredible amount of energy has gone into the fierce debate in mainstream Christian denominations over homosexuality. The display of passion that has been enlisted on both sides makes sense only if what we are experiencing is a fundamental debate in the Christian community about what it means to be human. Certainly no one would suggest that those who engage in homosexual activity are somehow less than human. Questions in the Church about what constitutes a human life are primarily being asked around the beginnings and endings of physical life, and at those times in which rational and emotional functions have either not yet emerged or are severely impaired — issues about which Scripture seems to have little interest. The debate in the Church over homosexuality, on the other hand, is not about what it means to be a human, but rather about what it means to live humanly — that is, how God intends for humans to behave. Scripture calls this a choosing of life or death, choosing good or evil.[35]

The arguments over whether or not any type of homosexual expression is acceptable within the Christian community have included psychological, sociological, and physiological data, which have sought to answer the question of whether or not some humans are hardwired as homosexuals and whether or not there is any perceived social or psychological damage associated with homosexual behavior. But even if it can be established that homosexual identity is preprogrammed, and even if the social and psychological sciences can pronounce their blessing on such unions, this hardly brings resolution to the question of whether or not homosexual behavior is acceptable for Christians — or, to use the language of Scripture, whether such behavior represents the choosing of "life" or "death," whether it is "good" or "evil." One might argue that the answer to Scripture's question depends upon which metaphor one chooses to use. Is homosexual orientation to be likened to a person's predisposition toward alcoholism? In that case, abstinence no doubt is the most life-giving course of action. The requirement of abstinence for a homosexual person is the official stance of most mainline denominations, which have placed any and all homosexual expression in the category of "sin" (i.e. choosing death and not life). But what if homosexual orientation should be likened to being left-handed? Regardless of the metaphorical comparison, however, the question before the Christian community is not what constitutes human beings or how we are predisposed genetically or sociologically, but how our Creator intends for us to behave. That is the fundamental anthropological question!

Since the scriptural witness, particularly as it is perceived through the Christ of Scripture, remains the foundational authority for Christians, one can hardly imagine how this matter will ever be resolved within the Christian community unless we can come to a consensus on a biblical approach to it. Unfortunately, the debate around Scripture has been more or less limited to those half-dozen texts that specifically refer to same-sex intercourse. Since without exception these references condemn it, Christians have dealt with these Scriptures in one of three ways. Many have interpreted the plain sense of the texts in the long tradition of the Church to mean that homosexual expression is a rejection of God's intention for human sexuality and therefore a sin, unacceptable in the life of the Christian community. Others have rejected the Old Testament texts outright as being a part of the "holiness code," which Christians have not observed since New Testament times, and have argued that the remaining New Testament references to homosexual unions are not about homosexuality per se, but are references to same-sex pedophilia and sexual promiscuity as practiced within the Hellenistic culture of the times. Still others have discarded the biblical condemnation of same-sex intercourse altogether, arguing that the biblical writers did not understand homosexual orientation as we do today. While the Bible's authors perceived homosexual acts as evidence of willful rebellion against God's intention for one's sexuality, today we understand homosexuality within the framework of a sexual orientation over which we have no fundamental control. Therefore, they argue, those texts referring to homosexual acts cannot be any more authoritative for modern Christians than the descriptions of a three-story universe through which the biblical authors perceived the cosmos.

The problem, it seems to me, with these three basic approaches to the several texts that refer to homosexual acts is that not one of them offers a sufficient biblical anthropology within which to critique homosexuality itself. While some have argued that the Genesis creation account gives a very clear anthropological framework for sexual expression within the created order of "male and female,"[36] it is not at all clear why one should exclude every single sexual expression outside the heterosexual ordering of it. A simple distinction between "male and female" can hardly account for *all* the variation in "plumbing" and genetic makeup expressed in the creation of humans. Whether such variations as occur within the natural order are understood as "brokenness" or as the intentional act of the Creator, they are a fact of our existence. To dismiss them outright simply because they do not fit a straightforward category of "male" and "female" is like saying to someone born without legs that unless you can walk on your own two feet, you have no business going anywhere.

While I have no illusion that my proposal in this paper will end the debate in the church over homosexuality, I would suggest that a conversation around the larger themes of Scripture as to how we are called by God to fulfill our human destiny would be more productive than most of the discussion on the matter so far. I will here attempt to lay out the basic outlines of a biblical anthropology based on this assumption: fundamental to what it means to be human is a God-given vocation to live responsibility within a twofold relationship, the relationship with God and the relationship with one's fellow human beings. I readily acknowledge that my argument is rather simple and takes a broad brush to Scripture. It may well overlook aspects of the text that have a significant bearing on the issue. Yet I would hope that by looking at the question of homosexuality as it is informed by a biblical anthropology, we might bring to bear some additional insight on an issue that has polarized the Christian community.

The Twofold Relationship

In both Matthew and Mark, Jesus tells us that the twofold command to "love God and to love one's neighbor" sums up what it means to fulfill our human destiny as God intended. In Matthew's Gospel this command is described as the sum total of all that the law and the prophets require.[37] In Luke, Jesus tells us that if we follow this twofold command we will "live."[38] The Old Syriac version puts the verb "live" in the present tense, so that obeying the twofold command cannot be taken as a quid pro quo, but should be understood as a participation in life itself; it literally reads, "do this and you are living."[39] From these two texts, one could argue that Jesus understood that what it means to live humanly is summarized by this twofold relationship and the unique requirements of each. Following the tradition of Hebrew Scripture, Jesus does not define the human being metaphysically but relationally. His anthropology is discerned within the framework of these two overarching relationships, which are first defined in the Genesis creation stories and then further developed within the biblical narrative.

In the first chapters of Genesis, we are offered an anthropocentric account of creation, which provides an overarching myth for the entire biblical story. In it the human is described exclusively in relational terms. The text defines the human (male and female) by two all-encompassing relationships. The first is the relationship of the human creature to God as his/her creator. The second arises from the vocation given to the human creature by his/her creator in relationship to the rest of the world's creatures.

Concerning the first relationship, the writer of Genesis simply assumes that the very fact of creation requires human obedience to the will of the Creator. In the story, the Creator grants unlimited freedom to the human within the context of creation, with the single exception of one seemingly arbitrary limit. In the construct of that limit the human could choose either "life" or "death," and discern either "good" or "evil" within the relational categories of obedience or disobedience to God. This relationship and its requirements provide the backdrop for the entire life of the human creature within the biblical story.

The second relationship that the text describes is the human's tie to the rest of the created order, specifically the animal kingdom. In this relationship the human creature is given his/her vocation by God and by that exhibits his/her "likeness" to God. The writer of Genesis appears to link the phrase "being made in God's likeness" with the human vocation of dominion over the other creatures.[40] In its commentary on this, Psalm 8 also links humanity's God-given vocation of dominion over the other creatures with God's dominion over humanity.[41] In addition, the Psalmist defines the "dominion" that God demonstrates in relationship to humanity as characterized by being "mindful of" and "caring for." In the Genesis creation myth, the human expresses his/her vocational role of dominion by naming the animals. As a characterization of dominion, the human creature (male and female) is commanded to "be fruitful and multiply and subdue" Creation.

In the first chapter of Genesis, man and woman are undifferentiated, but as the narrative unfolds in subsequent chapters, the "bone of my bones and flesh of my flesh" becomes more and more the "other." We recognize this first in the naming of the woman as one who was taken "out of man," and we can see it later in the ascribing of blame. Finally the ultimate differentiation between humans is portrayed by the story of the killing of Abel by his brother, Cain. As the differentiation between humans is developed in the biblical narrative, the writer shows less and less interest in the relationship of the human to the animal creatures; the concern of the narrative turns more and more to the ethical implications of the relationships between human beings themselves. In the trajectory taken by the ensuing chapters of Genesis, it becomes clear that the relationships between humans supplant the relationship between the human creature and the animals as a primary definition of what it means to fulfill the human vocation. The Torah, the wisdom literature, the prophetic writings, and the New Testament books all follow suit in this regard. Jesus even implies in the Gospels that to "care for" (to have dominion over) the animals is God's task rather than that of humanity.[42] Instead, Jesus clearly emphasizes the human responsibility to care for other humans, particularly those in need. By embracing the summation of the Jewish religious law in the words "You shall love the Lord your God with all your heart, and with all your soul, and with all your strength, and with all your mind; and your neighbor as yourself"[43] as the fullest expression of human living, Jesus reaffirms the emphasis of the Hebrew Scriptures, which characterize human life by these two overarching relationships, the relationship to God and the relationship to other humans. Only by properly ordering these two relationships does one fully realize one's humanity.

While the early chapters of Genesis provide an overarching myth for the entire biblical story, the rest of Scripture's narrative makes little to no reference to its creation account until the New Testament, and even there the references are sparse.[44] Still, the Genesis myth, and the two overarching relationships by which it defines human life could be said to serve as a common, unifying theme of the entire Bible. The biblical writers had little interest in metaphysical categories; instead they described the human primarily in relational terms. The word "righteousness" is applied over 600 times in the Bible to those whose relationships are rightly ordered. The term first surfaces in Genesis 6 as a description of Noah, in contrast to the other humans who are wicked (i.e., those whose relationships are not right). It might also be argued that Scripture further develops the concept of righteousness by using the terms "holiness" and "justice," with holiness pertaining primarily to one's being within the sphere of a relationship with God, and justice describing one's proper relationship toward one's fellow human.[45] Around these two concepts, which are shaped by the two distinct foci of human relationship, God and other humans, grows a body of specific requirements and expectations.

Human Sexuality and the Twofold Relationship

William Countryman contends that what emerges from a study of the Bible's teachings on sex is a twofold sexual ethic originating in the Hebrew Scriptures and transformed by the New Testament authors. One part is a property ethic; its cardinal sin is greed, leading one to trespass on one's neighbor's property. The other part is a purity ethic, against which the fundamental offense is "uncleanness" or a violation of the holiness code.[46] This twofold sexual ethic appears to correspond to the twofold command to love God and neighbor, which is transformed first by the witness of Old Testament prophets, then by Jesus himself, and finally within the early Christian community into an ethic that makes neighborly concern the supreme example of the behavior that leads to life and honors one's relationship to God, and in effect displaces the purity ethic. If in fact homosexual expression per se is framed as a "holiness" issue, monogamous homosexual relationships could well find a place within the Christian community as an acceptable expression of sexuality, solely on the basis of a property ethic. On the other hand, if homosexual expression in and of itself is simply a matter of "holiness," why is it that those Scripture texts attributed to the apostle Paul are the very ones that appear to preclude all homosexual relationships from being lived out within the Christian community? It was Paul, after all, who, according to Acts, led the fight for the full inclusion of Gentiles in the Church by arguing that the purity requirements that reflected the proper ordering of a Jew's relationship to God did not apply to the Gentile Christian and were hardly a prerequisite for participating in the life-giving reality of the Gospel. William Countryman argues that while Paul did speak of "impurity" fairly often in compiling his lists of vices, he always used it in a metaphorical sense and never as a simple and unambiguous reference to physical impurity of a sexual kind.[47] Furthermore, Countryman argues that in the first chapter of his letter to the Romans, Paul was in fact describing the "uncleanness" of the Gentile culture (which he does not equate with sin), which was a direct result of the root sin of idolatry.[48]

While the merits of Countryman's argument can certainly be questioned, thoughtful Christians must undoubtedly give attention to the distinction that the New Testament writers make between the Old Testament's two categories of sin reflected in the twofold command to love God and neighbor. The New Testament witness does not allow us to simply lump these two (which the Torah defines as sin) together indiscriminately, and demands that we place the value of neighborliness as the highest expression of human behavior in the choosing of life over death, good over evil.

The question the homosexual person puts before the Christian community is similar to the one asked Philip by the Ethiopian eunuch, who was prohibited on the basis of his sexual organ from participating in Temple worship:[49] "What is to prevent me from being baptized?"[50] Certainly there are many things that would prevent a person from being baptized. Today the question before the Christian community is whether or not a monogamous homosexual relationship is one of them.

APPENDIX

2000-2001 Pastor-Theologian Program

Center of Theological Inquiry
Princeton, New Jersey

Resource Theologians

Carl Braaten
Center for Catholic and Evangelical Theology
Sun City West, Arizona

Brian Daley
University of Notre Dame
South Bend, Indiana

Gabriel Fackre
Andover Newton Theological School
Newton Centre, Massachusetts

Beverly Roberts Gaventa
Princeton Theological Seminary
Princeton, New Jersey

Shirley Guthrie
Columbia Theological Seminary
Decatur, Georgia

J. Wentzel van Huyssteen
Princeton Theological Seminary
Princeton, New Jersey

Robert W. Jenson
Center of Theological Inquiry
Princeton, New Jersey

Donald H. Juel
Princeton Theological Seminary
Princeton, New Jersey

Bruce Marshall
Perkins School of Theology
Dallas, Texas

James L. Mays
Union Theological Seminary
Richmond, Virginia

Alexander McKelway
Davidson College
Davidson, North Carolina

Daniel L. Migliori
Princeton Theological Seminary
Princeton, New Jersey

Margaret Odell
St. Olaf College
Northfield, Minnesota

Mark P. Reasoner
Bethel College
St. Paul, Minnesota

R. Kendall Soulen
Wesley Theological Seminary
Washington, District of Columbia

Regional Seminar Conveners

Cynthia A. Jarvis — Northeast
The Presbyterian Church of Chestnut Hill
Philadelphia, Pennsylvania

James D. Miller — South Central
First Presbyterian Church
Tulsa, Oklahoma

Bruce Rigdon — North Central
Grosse Pointe Memorial Church
Grosse Pointe Farms, Michigan

John Stapleton — Southeast
St. John's United Methodist Church
Aiken, South Carolina

Virgil F. Thompson, Jr. — West
Bethlehem Lutheran Church
Spokane, Washington

Pastor-Theologians

Barbara J. Archer
First Christian Church
Butte, Montana

Byron C. Bangert
Presbytery of Ohio Valley
Bloomington, Indiana

Joseph A. Bassett
The First Church in Chestnut Hill
Chestnut Hill, Massachusetts

Joseph Carle
Chapel Hill Presbyterian Church
Blue Springs, Missouri

Kenneth H. Carter, Jr.
Mount Tabor United Methodist Church
Winston-Salem, North Carolina

John R. Christopherson
First Lutheran Church
Sioux Falls, South Dakota

Deborah Rahn Clemens
Frieden's United Church of Christ
Sumneytown, Pennsylvania

Richard J. Coleman
Interim Ministry
Pembroke, Massachusetts

J. Randy Cooper
First and Trinity United Methodist Churches
Henderson, Tennessee

Jennifer E. Copeland
Duke University Wesley Fellowship
Durham, North Carolina

Richard R. Crocker
Central Presbyterian Church
Montclair, New Jersey

Thomas W. Currie III
First Presbyterian Church
Kerrville, Texas

Robert W. Dahlen
Goodridge Area Lutheran Parish
Goodridge, Minnesota

F. Harry Daniel
First Presbyterian Church
Dalton, Georgia

Joseph H. DeRoulhac, Jr.
The First Baptist Church of Redlands
Redlands, California

Douglas L. Dobson
Holy Cross Lutheran Church
Salem, Oregon

Barry H. Downing
Northminster Presbyterian Church
Endwell, New York

Jeffrey C. Eaton
Emanuel Evangelical Lutheran Church
New Brunswick, New Jersey

Mateen A. Elass
Immanuel Presbyterian Church
Warrenville, Illinois

Barry A. Ensign-George
Springville and Linn Grove Presbyterian Churches
Springville, Iowa

Pamela R. Fickenscher
The Spirit Garage
Minneapolis, Minnesota

Douglas K. Fletcher
Westlake Hills Presbyterian Church
Austin, Texas

Richard L. Floyd
First Church of Christ in Pittsfield, Congregational
Pittsfield, Massachusetts

Shirley R. Funk
Lake Edge Lutheran Church
Madison, Wisconsin

James A. Gilchrist
Second Presbyterian Church
Carlisle, Pennsylvania

Sonja M. Hagander
Augsburg College Campus Ministry
Minneapolis, Minnesota

Robert A. Hausman
The Lutheran Church of the Resurrection
St. Paul, Minnesota

David Henderson
St. Paul's Episcopal Church
Steamboat Springs, Colorado

Scott Hoezee
Calvin Christian Reformed Church
Grand Rapids, Michigan

Jonathan L. Jenkins
Holy Spirit Lutheran Church
Lancaster, Pennsylvania

John Mark Jones
Trinity United Methodist Church
North Myrtle Beach, South Carolina

Albert H. Keller
Circular Congregational Church, UCC
Charleston, South Carolina

Adelia Kelso
Northminster Presbyterian Church
Pearl River, Louisiana

Jim Kitchens
Davis Community Church
Davis, California

Joel E. Kok
Trinity Christian Reformed Church
Broomall, Pennsylvania

Rebecca Kuiken
Stone Church of Willow Glen
San Jose, California

Donald M. Mackenzie
University Congregational United Church of Christ
Seattle, Washington

Paul D. Matheny
Union Theological Seminary
Republic of the Philippines

J. Harold McKeithen, Jr.
Hidenwood Presbyterian Church
Newport News, Virginia

Thomas D. McKnight
Moreland Presbyterian Church
Portland, Oregon

Allen C. McSween, Jr.
Fourth Presbyterian Church
Greenville, South Carolina

David D. Miles
Austin Presbyterian Theological Seminary
Austin, Texas

Bruce K. Modahl
Grace Lutheran Church
River Forest, Illinois

W. Rush Otey III
First Presbyterian Church
Pensacola, Florida

Thomas A. Renquist
Lord of the Hills Lutheran Church
Aurora, Colorado

Robert S. Rice
First Presbyterian Church
Norman, Oklahoma

John B. Rogers, Jr.
Covenant Presbyterian Church
Charlotte, North Carolina

John Rollefson
Lord of Light Lutheran Church
Ann Arbor, Michigan

Charles T. Rush, Jr.
Christ Church
Summit, New Jersey

Charles M. Smith
United Methodist Church
Rocky Mount, North Carolina

Samuel H. Speers
Vassar College
Poughkeepsie, New York

Erik J. Strand
Edina Community Lutheran Church
Edina, Minnesota

Laird J. Stuart
Calvary Presbyterian Church
San Francisco, California

Hamilton Coe Throckmorton
Barrington Congregational Church
Barrington, Rhode Island

Charles Valenti-Hein
Memorial Presbyterian Church
Appleton, Wisconsin

J. Barry Vaughn
St. Peter's Episcopal Church
Philadelphia, Pennsylvania

F. Joseph Wahlin
Holy Shepherd Lutheran Church
Lakewood, Colorado

Anita R. Warner
Advent Lutheran Church
Morgan Hill, California

Paul A. Wee
The Luther Center
Wittenberg, Germany

Ken C. Williams
Rockland Community Church
Golden, Colorado

Notes

PART ONE

CHAPTER I

Section 1

1. Udo Schnelle, *The Human Condition* (Minneapolis: Fortress Press, 1996), 5.

2. Paul Achtemeier, *Romans* (Atlanta: John Knox Press, 1985), 108-9.

3. James D. G. Dunn, "Romans 7:14-25 in the Theology of Paul" in *Theologische Zeitschrift,* Vol. 31, 1975.

4. Dunn, "Romans 7:14-25," 258.

5. C. H. Dodd, *Romans,* Moffatt New Testament Commentary, ed. James Moffatt (London: Hodder and Stoughton, 1932), 107. Also F. F. Bruce, *The Epistle of Paul to the Romans* (London: Tyndale Press, 1963), 147-156.

6. Ernst Käsemann, *Commentary on Romans,* trans. and ed. Geoffrey W. Bromiley (Grand Rapids: Eerdmans, 1980), 197.

7. Anders Nygren, *Commentary on Romans* (Philadelphia: Muhlenberg Press, 1949), 293-94.

8. C. E. B. Cranfield, *The Epistle to the Romans,* 2 vols., International Critical Commentary (Edinburgh: T&T Clark, 1975), 1:356.

Section 2

9. Philip Edgcumbe Hughes, *The True Image: The Origin and Destiny of Man in Christ* (Grand Rapids: Eerdmans, 1989), 15.

10. Karl Barth, *Church Dogmatics,* III/2 (Edinburgh: T&T Clark, 1960), 3.

11. John Williamson Nevin, "Cur Deus Homo?" *The Mercersburg Review* 3 (1851): 223.

12. Nevin, "Cur Deus Homo?" 235.

13. Barth, *Church Dogmatics,* III/2, 228.

14. Karl Barth, *The Epistle to the Philippians* (London: SCM Press, 1962).

15. Nevin, "Cur Deus Homo?" 205.

Section 3

16. See John B. Rogers Jr., "The Book That Reads Us," *Interpretation: A Journal of Bible and Theology,* October 1985.

17. Walter Brueggemann, *Genesis* (Atlanta: John Knox Press, 1982), 41.

18. Brueggemann, *Genesis,* 54.

19. James L. Mays, *Psalms* (Louisville: John Knox Press, 1994), 199.

20. Mays, *Psalms,* 200.

21. Mays, *Psalms,* 201-2.

22. Paul J. Achtemeier, *Romans* (Atlanta: John Knox, 1985), 96.

23. Achtemeier, *Romans,* 39.

24. Fleming Rutledge, *The Bible and the New York Times* (Grand Rapids: Eerdmans, 1998), 89.

25. Douglas John Hall, *Professing the Faith: Christian Theology in a North American Context* (Minneapolis: Fortress Press, 1993), 216.

26. Daniel L. Migliori, *Faith Seeking Understanding* (Grand Rapids: Eerdmans, 1991), 130.

Section 4

27. Wilhelm Vischer, unpublished lectures, Faculté de Théologie Protestante, Montpellier, France, 1963-64.

28. Hans-Walter Wolff, *Anthropology of the Old Testament* (Minneapolis: Fortress, 1996), 38.

29. James L. Mays, *Psalms* (Louisville: John Knox Press, 1944), 13.

30. Philip Hefner, *The Human Factor: Evolution, Culture, and Religion* (Minneapolis: Augsburg-Fortress, 1993).

31. Hefner, *Human Factor,* 46.

CHAPTER II

Section 5

1. John Leith, from a mimeographed sermon from the late 1970s entitled "The Church as the People of God." It was given to me by Allen McSween.

2. Robert F. Evans, *Pelagius: Inquiries and Reappraisals* (New York: Seabury, 1968), 79-111. See also Evans, *Four Letters of Pelagius* (London: Black, 1968); J. N. D. Kelly, *Early Christian Doctrines* (New York: Harper and Row, 1960); James Orr, *The Progress of Dogma* (Grand Rapids: Eerdmans, 1960); and especially *The Nicene and Post-Nicene Fathers: First Series,* Volume 5, ed. Philip Schaff (Albany, Ore.: Books for the Ages Software, 1997).

3. Henry Bettenson, ed., *Documents of the Christian Church* (London: Oxford, 1963), 52.

4. Bettenson, ed., *Documents of the Christian Church,* 52.

5. Peter Brown, *Augustine of Hippo: A Biography* (Berkeley and Los Angeles: University of California, 1969), 346-47.

6. Jaroslav Pelikan, *Development of Christian Doctrine: Some Historical Prolegomena* (New Haven: Yale, 1969), 74-75.

7. R. C. Sproul, *Augustine and Pelagius,* found at www.geocities.com/Heartland/9170/SPROUL1.HTM.

8. Augustine, *On Grace,* in *The Later Christian Fathers,* ed. Henry Bettenson (London: Oxford, 1979), 204.

9. Augustine, *On Grace,* 205.

10. Augustine, *On Grace,* 208.

11. Augustine, *On Grace,* 218-19.

12. Augustine, *Admonition and Grace,* quoted in Warren Thomas Smith, *Augustine: His Life and Thought* (Atlanta: John Knox, 1980), 134.

Section 6

13. Some 1600 years later, this musing still finds an echoing voice in the thought of Hans Jonas. See his *The Phenomenon of Life* (Chicago: The University of Chicago Press, 1982), 183.

14. Augustine, *The Confessions,* IV/5 and X/16.

15. Similarly, Warren S. Brown observes, "Probably nothing in the known universe is as complex as human nature." *Whatever Happened to the Soul? Scientific and Theological Portraits of Human Nature,* ed. Warren S. Brown, Nancey Murphy, and H. Newton Malony (Minneapolis: Fortress Press, 1988), 227. Similarly, Reinhold Niebuhr begins his famous Gifford Lectures with this observation: "Man has always been his own most vexing problem. How shall he think of himself? Every affirmation which he may make about his stature, virtue, or place in the cosmos becomes involved in contradictions when fully analyzed." *The Nature and Destiny of Man,* Vol. 1 (New York: Charles Scribner's Sons, 1941), 1.

16. James M. Childs, Jr., *Christian Anthropology and Ethics* (Philadelphia: Fortress Press, 1978), 2.

17. Bruce Birch and Larry Rasmussen contend that "The moral significance of character resides in part then in the fact that our 'being' shapes our 'seeing' and the way we see things gives us a particular outlook and orientation toward life," in *Bible and Ethics in the Christian Life* (Minneapolis: Augsburg Publishing, 1976), 89. Certainly "being" not only shapes our "doing"; "doing" shapes "being" — as Aristotle stated long ago in his *Nicomachean Ethics.* However, the premise we will argue for in this essay is that the question "Who are we as humans?" stands necessarily prior to, though not independent of, the question "How or what are we to do for, or on behalf of, what it means to be human?" The relationship of being and doing here is one of subordinate interdependency and not a coordinate serial progression.

18. It is rather propitious that the theme for Trinity Institute's 32nd National Conference in New York City is "What Does It Mean to Be Human?" This question is being intentionally and carefully examined by various institutes and centers; the Church needs to examine it as well.

19. Paul Ramsey, *Fabricated Man* (New Haven: Yale University Press, 1970), 151.

20. Pelagius, "Letter to Demetrias," in J. Patout Burns, ed., *Theological Anthropology* (Philadelphia: Fortress Press, 1978), 53 (emphasis added).

21. For example, a recent release from the Associated Press reads, "The man wanted in the 1998 slaying of a Buffalo [New York] abortion doctor who was cut down by a sniper's bullet in his kitchen was captured in France on Thursday." *Bozeman Daily Chronicle,* Friday, March 10, 2001. The bombing of abortion clinics or shooting staff members is a perfect case in point of how a given understanding of what constitutes the human gives rise to certain actions that are then considered justifiable.

22. James B. Nelson, *Rediscovering the Person in Medical Care* (Minneapolis: Augsburg Publishing, 1976), 21.

23. Paul Ramsey, *The Patient as Person* (New Haven: Yale University Press, 1970); see esp. xi-xviii.

24. James B. Nelson, *Human Medicine* (Minneapolis: Augsburg Publishing, 1973); see esp. 17-28.

25. William F. May, *Human Existence — Medicine and Ethics* (Chicago: Franciscan Herald Press, 1977); see esp. 1-9. See also May's *The Physician's Covenant* (Philadelphia: The Westminster Press, 1983).

26. Joseph Fletcher, *Humanhood: Essays in Biomedical Ethics* (Buffalo, New York: Prometheus Books, 1979); see esp. 7-19.

27. Ronald Cole-Turner, ed., *Human Cloning: Religious Responses* (Louisville, Kentucky: Westminster John Knox Press, 1997).

28. Ted Peters, *Playing God? Genetic Determinism and Human Freedom* (New York: Routledge, 1997).

29. Richard A. McCormick, "Human Significance and Christian Significance," in *Norm and Context in Christian Ethics,* ed. Gene H. Outka and Paul Ramsey (New York: Charles Scribner's Sons, 1968), 247-49. For a magisterial rehearsal of how various periods of history inform one's understanding of what constitutes the human, see Reinhold Niebuhr's *The Nature and Destiny of Man,* Vol. 1 (New York: Charles Scribner's Sons, 1964), esp. 1-300.

30. Abraham Heschel, *Who Is Man?* (Stanford: Stanford University Press, 1978), 29-30.

Section 7

31. The Roman Catholic/Presbyterian-Reformed Consultation Washington-Princeton, *Ethics and the Search for Christian Unity: Two Statements.* Washington, D.C.: United States Catholic Conference, 1980.

32. *Ethics and the Search for Christian Unity,* 43.

CHAPTER III

Section 8

1. *New York Times,* May 1, 2001. Dolphins may be capable, like apes and humans, of self-recognition.

Section 9

2. "Toward a Feminist Theology," *The Christian Century,* August 2, 1972.

3. "Toward a Feminist Theology."

4. Peter C. Hodgson and Robert H. King, *Christian Theology: An Introduction to Its Traditions and Tasks* (Philadelphia: Fortress Press, 1982), 148.

5. Webster's *Third New International Dictionary* corroborates this point with its second definition for anthropology, namely, "religious teaching about the origin, nature, and destiny of man [sic] from the perspective of his [sic] relation to God."

6. The reformulation of theology, more or less along the lines to be suggested here, is also an intellectual necessity. I am in substantial agreement with the well-known scientist and theologian Arthur Peacocke, both in his specific proposals for theological reformulation and in his more general assessment of the current state of church theology: "There is an increasingly alarming dissonance between the language of devotion, liturgies and doctrine and what people perceive themselves to be, and to be becoming, in the light of the cognitive science and in the world described by the 'historical' sciences (cosmology, geology, biology) in the 'epic of evolution.' . . . We require an open, revisable, exploratory, radical (dare I say it?) Liberal theology. This may well be unfashionable among Christians who seem everywhere to be retreating into their fortresses of classical Protestant Evangelicalism, traditional (Anglo-)Catholicism and/or so-called 'biblical theology.' Nevertheless, transition to such a theology is, in my view, actually *unavoidable* if Christians in the West and, I suspect, eventually elsewhere are not to degenerate in the next millennium into an esoteric society internally communing with itself and thereby failing to be the transmitter of its 'good news' (the evangel) to the universal *(Catholicos)* world." "Science and the Future of Theology — Critical Issues," *Reflections* (Center of Theological Inquiry) 3 (Autumn 2000): 40-41.

7. "Violence Against Women: The Theological Dimension," *Christianity and Crisis,* May 30, 1983, p. 206. Cf. Anne O'Hara Graff: "Today the exploration of women's experience is a critical corrective and constructive element within the revelatory creative movement of tradition itself. . . . [T]he resource of women's experience will highlight the systemic distortions of Scripture and the multiple theological traditions that have done harm to women." Graff, ed., *In the Embrace of God: Feminist Approaches to Theological Anthropology* (Maryknoll, N.Y.: Orbis Books, 1995), 83-84.

Section 10

8. Leon and Amy Kass, quoted in *Mars Hill Audio Journal* 46 (September/October 2000).

9. Mary Shelley, *Frankenstein* (New York: Penguin Putnam, 2000), 38-89.

10. Shelley, *Frankenstein,* 110.

11. Harold Bloom, "Afterword" to *Frankenstein* (New York: Penguin Putnam, 2000), 202.

12. Bloom, "Afterword," 209.

13. The most powerful example of this I've seen in recent years is the film "Alien Resurrection," which contains some horrific examples of failure at human cloning. Even the "successful" clone is chilling.

14. Paul Santmire, *Nature Reborn: The Ecological and Cosmic Promise of Christian Theology* (Philadelphia: Fortress Press, 2000). Santmire is particularly critical of those who would avoid fall-redemption language, as if the *idea* of the Fall is responsible for the results of the Fall (see pp. 20-25).

15. Santmire, *Nature Reborn,* 94.

16. Santmire, *Nature Reborn,* 94.

PART TWO

CHAPTER IV

Section 11

1. John F. Haught, *God After Darwin: A Theology of Evolution* (Boulder, Colo.: Westview Press, 2000), 70.

2. Haught, *God After Darwin,* 77.

Section 12

3. Frederick E. Crowe, "Complacency and Concern in the Risen Life," *Lonergan Workshop* 13 (1997): 17-32.

4. Crowe, "Complacency and Concern," 20.

5. Robert Jenson, *On Thinking the Human: Resolutions of Difficult Notions* (Grand Rapids: Eerdmans, 2003), Chapter One, "Thinking Death."

6. Jenson, *On Thinking the Human.*

7. Jenson, *On Thinking the Human.*

Section 13

8. Eugene Fontinell, *Self, God, and Immortality* (Philadelphia: Temple University Press, 1986), 7-8.

9. Edward O. Wilson, *On Human Nature* (Cambridge: Harvard University Press, 1978), 2.

10. Wilson, *On Human Nature,* 176.

11. Wilson, *On Human Nature,* 171.

12. Wilson, *On Human Nature,* 206-8.

13. John Hick, *Death and Eternal Life* (Louisville: Westminster/John Knox Press, 1994).

14. Paul Badham, *Christian Beliefs About Life After Death* (London: Macmillan Press Ltd., 1976).

15. Badham, *Christian Beliefs,* 125-32.

16. Badham, *Christian Beliefs,* 126.

17. Badham, *Christian Beliefs,* 127.

18. Badham, *Christian Beliefs,* 110.

19. Keith Campbell, *Body and Mind* (London: Macmillan, 1971), 91.

20. Warren Brown, Nancey Murphy, and H. Newton Malony, *Whatever Happened to the Soul?* (Minneapolis: Fortress Press, 1998), 99.

21. Brown, Murphy, and Malony, *Whatever Happened to the Soul?* 102.

22. Brown, Murphy, and Malony, *Whatever Happened to the Soul?* 102.

23. Brown, Murphy, and Malony, *Whatever Happened to the Soul?* 102.

24. Brown, Murphy, and Malony, *Whatever Happened to the Soul?* 102.

CHAPTER V

Section 14

1. David F. Ford, *Self and Salvation: Being Transformed* (Cambridge: Cambridge University Press, 1999), 17-44, summarized on 65.

2. Ford, *Self and Salvation,* 9.

Section 15

3. Tertullian, *On Baptism,* trans. Ernest Evans (London: SPCK, 1964), 8-9.

4. Tertullian, *On Baptism,* 17.

5. Tertullian, *On Baptism,* 17.

6. E. A. Yarnold, *The Awe-Inspiring Rites of Initiation: The Origins of the RCIA* (Collegeville, Minn.: The Liturgical Press, 1994), 155.

7. Yarnold, *Awe-Inspiring Rites,* 25.

8. Yarnold, *Awe-Inspiring Rites,* 119.

9. Yarnold, *Awe-Inspiring Rites,* 187-88.

10. Yarnold, *Awe-Inspiring Rites,* 101.

11. E. C. Whitaker, *Documents of the Baptismal Liturgy* (London: SPCK, 1960), 4.

12. Yarnold, *Awe-Inspiring Rites,* 34.

13. Cf. Justin Martyr ("this washing is called enlightenment") and Cyril of Jerusalem ("O ye who are being enlightened!") in Whitaker, *Documents,* 2, 24.

14. Quoted in Frederik van der Meer, *Augustine the Bishop: Religion and Society at the Dawn of the Middle Ages,* trans. Brian Battershaw and G. R. Lamb (New York: Harper Torchbooks, 1965), 363.

15. Whitaker, *Documents,* 7.

16. Yarnold, *Awe-Inspiring Rites,* 76-77.

17. Alexander Schmemann, *Of Water and the Spirit: A Liturgical Study of Baptism* (Crestwood, N.Y.: St. Vladimir's Seminary Press, 1974), 23-24.

18. Robert Jenson, *Visible Words* (Philadelphia: Fortress Press, 1978), 155.

19. Whitaker, *Documents*, 4.

20. Yarnold, *Awe-Inspiring Rites*, 70.

21. Yarnold, *Awe-Inspiring Rites*, 162.

22. Yarnold, *Awe-Inspiring Rites*, 162-63.

23. Whitaker, *Documents*, 80.

24. Yarnold, *Awe-Inspiring Rites*, 197.

25. Jenson, *Systematic Theology*, Vol. 2 (New York: Oxford University Press, 1997), 162.

Section 16

26. Michael Welker, "The Reign of God," *Theology Today* 49 (1993): 514.

27. Walter Brueggemann, *The Message of the Psalms: A Theological Commentary* (Minneapolis: Augsburg, 1984), 12.

28. Robert Jenson, *The Triune Identity* (Philadelphia: Fortress, 1982), 119.

CHAPTER VI

Section 17

1. Carl Sandburg, *Poems of the Midwest* (Cleveland: World Publishing Company, 1946), 47.

2. Sharon Daloz Parks, *Big Questions, Worthy Dreams* (San Francisco: Jossey-Bass, 2000), 148.

3. Parks believes that focusing on dependence gives us access to what a person feels. In this, she draws on the works of William Weyerhaeuser.

4. Parks, *Big Questions, Worthy Dreams*, 83.

5. Parks, *Big Questions, Worthy Dreams*, 84.

6. David Brooks, "The Next Ruling Class: Meet the Organization Kid," *The Atlantic Monthly*, April 2001.

7. Brooks, "The Next Ruling Class."

8. Brooks, "The Next Ruling Class."

9. Brooks, "The Next Ruling Class."

10. Brooks, "The Next Ruling Class."

11. "Augsburg 2004: Extending the Vision," available at http://www.augsburg.edu/augsburg2004/augsburg2004.pdf.

12. Romans 6 shows the accusing work of the law and the new life in the gospel.

13. *Luther's Works*, 55 vols. (Philadelphia: Fortress; St. Louis: Concordia, 1955-76), 26:6, 14, 35, 116-17, 306-15, 334.

14. *The Precious and Sacred Writings of Martin Luther*, ed. John Lenker, 10 vols. (Minneapolis: Lutherans in All Lands Co., 1905), 10:242.

15. Luther, *The Table Talk of Martin Luther* (London: George Bell and Sons, 1895), 362-63.

16. *Intersections,* Fall 2000, 5.

17. *Luther's Works,* 45:127.

18. Gustaf Wingren, *Luther on Vocation* (Philadelphia: Muhlenberg Press, 1957), 68.

19. Wingren, *Luther on Vocation,* 71.

20. H. Richard Niebuhr, *Christ and Culture* (New York: Harper and Row, 1951), 179.

Section 19

21. Walter Wink, ed., *Homosexuality and Christian Faith: Questions for the Churches* (Minneapolis: Fortress, 1999), 33.

22. Choon-Leong Seow, ed., *Homosexuality and Christian Community* (Louisville: Westminster/John Knox, 1996), 1, 24.

23. Seow, ed., *Homosexuality and Christian Community,* 22.

24. Seow, ed., *Homosexuality and Christian Community,* 60.

25. Robert Jenson, *Systematic Theology,* Vol. 2 (New York: Oxford University Press, 1999), 93.

26. Paul Jersild, *Spirit Ethics: Scripture and the Moral Life* (Minneapolis: Fortress, 2000), 60.

27. Jersild, *Spirit Ethics,* 135, 137.

28. Richard Hays, *The Moral Vision of the New Testament* (San Francisco: Harper Collins, 1996), 399.

29. Hays, *Moral Vision,* 399.

30. Seow, ed., *Homosexuality and Christian Community,* 72.

31. Karen Bloomquist and John Stumme, eds., *The Promise of Lutheran Ethics* (Minneapolis: Fortress, 1998), 165.

32. Seow, ed., *Homosexuality and Christian Community,* 57.

33. Paul Lehmann, *The Decalogue and a Human Future: The Meaning of the Commandments for Making and Keeping Human Life Human* (Grand Rapids: Eerdmans, 1995), 174.

34. Christian Scharen, *Married in the Sight of God: Theology, Ethics and Church Debates over Homosexuality* (Lanham, Md.: University Press of America, 2000), 55-92.

Section 20

35. Deuteronomy 30:15-19.

36. In his *Systematic Theology,* Robert Jenson states that "'homosexuality,' if it exists and whatever it is, cannot be attributed to creation." He argues for an anthropology based on the creation stories of Genesis and on sexual "plumbing," which dismisses homosexual expression as a legitimate option within God's created order (p. 93).

37. Matthew 22:40.

38. Luke 10:28.

39. Ken Bailey, *Through Peasant Eyes* (Grand Rapids: Eerdmans, 1980), 38.

40. Hans-Walter Wolff, *Anthropology of the Old Testament* (Philadelphia: Fortress Press, 1974), 159-62. (In *Church Dogmatics,* III/2 [Edinburgh: T&T Clark, 1960], 324, Karl Barth argues that the human's divine likeness is based on the fact that he/she is in relationship, just as God is.)

41. Wolff, *Anthropology of the Old Testament,* 226-27.

42. Matthew 6:26.

43. Luke 10:27.

44. It is curious that St. Augustine and the Gnostics are so preoccupied with particulars of the Genesis creation myth when the rest of the biblical writers all but ignore them.

45. It is not at all clear that "justice" and "holiness" are paired with "righteousness" in the same way. "Righteousness" and "justice" appear to be used interchangeably in the text, unlike "holiness," which connotes more of a spatial than an ethical relationship.

46. William Countryman, *Dirt, Greed and Sex* (Philadelphia: Fortress, 1988), ix.

47. Countryman, *Dirt, Greed and Sex,* 104-6.

48. Countryman, *Dirt, Greed and Sex,* 110-13. Countryman writes, "Paul's basic argument here runs thus: Idolatry was the root sin of Gentile culture. In the creation, God left ample evidence of his goodness, power, and divinity, so that any people should have known enough to worship and give thanks to him alone. The Gentiles, in the stupidity of their hearts, chose instead to worship 'a likeness of an image of a perishable human being and of birds and beasts and vermin' (1:23). This was a voluntary act, effected in full knowledge of its meaning; and it is the reason why 'God surrendered them in the desires of their hearts to uncleanness' (v. 24). Paul did not, of course, mean that every Gentile invented idolatry individually or that each began to experience homosexual desire as a direct result of individual sin. He was thinking in terms of Gentile culture as a whole, not of individuals: the original forebears of the Gentiles committed the sin of idolatry, in which their descendants, in the normal course of events, have followed them; and this is why God has also decreed that certain unclean practices are to be characteristic of their culture. Compare Paul's similar treatment of God's dealings with Israel as a nation in Romans 11:11-36."

49. Leviticus 21:18-20.

50. Acts 8:36.